ZIGGY®
COMES UP SHORT

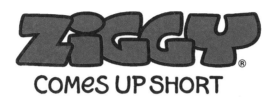

Recent *Ziggy* Books

Ziggy . . . A Rumor in His Own Time
A Day in the Life of Ziggy . . .
1-800-ZIGGY
My Life as a Cartoon
The Z Files
Ziggy's Divine Comedy
Get Ziggy with It
The Zen of Ziggy
Ziggy Goes Hollywood
Character Matters
Ziggy on Parade

Treasuries

Ziggy's Star Performances
The First 25 Years Are the Hardest!
Ziggy's Friends for Life
Ziggy's Gift
A Little Character Goes a Long Way

COMES UP SHORT

THE ICONIC ZIGGY IN HIS NEWEST COMIC COLLECTION

by Tom Wilson

**Andrews McMeel
Publishing, LLC**

Kansas City

08 09 10 11 12 TWP 10 9 8 7 6 5 4 3 2 1

ISBN-13: 978-0-7407-7371-6
ISBN-10: 0-7407-7371-2

Library of Congress Control Number: 2008922537

www.andrewsmcmeel.com

ATTENTION: SCHOOLS AND BUSINESSES

Andrews McMeel books are available at quantity discounts with bulk purchase for educational, business, or sales promotional use. For information, please write to: Special Sales Department, Andrews McMeel Publishing, LLC, 1130 Walnut Street, Kansas City, Missouri 64106.

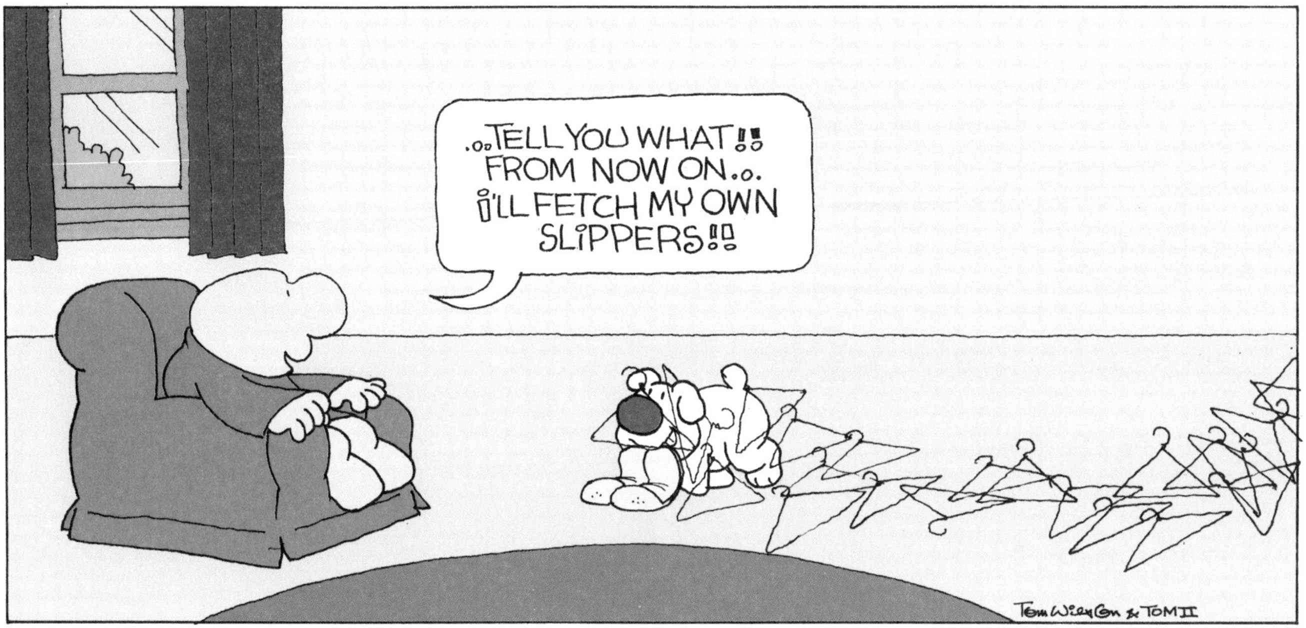
..TELL YOU WHAT!!
FROM NOW ON...
I'LL FETCH MY OWN
SLIPPERS!!
TOM WILSON & TOM II

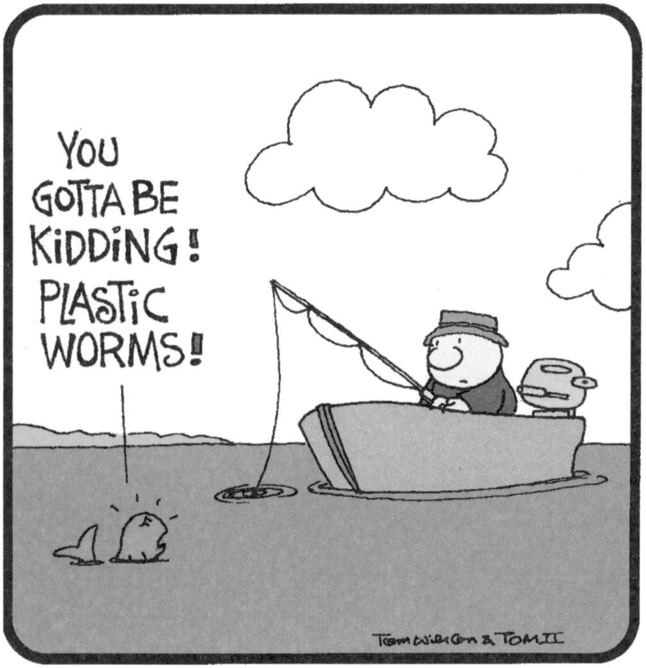
YOU GOTTA BE KIDDING! PLASTIC WORMS!
TOM WILSON & TOM II

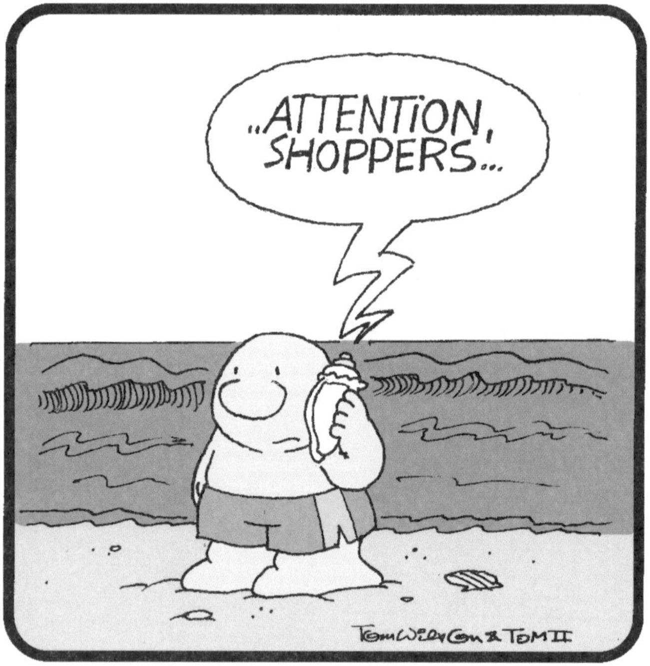
..ATTENTION, SHOPPERS...
TOM WILSON & TOM II

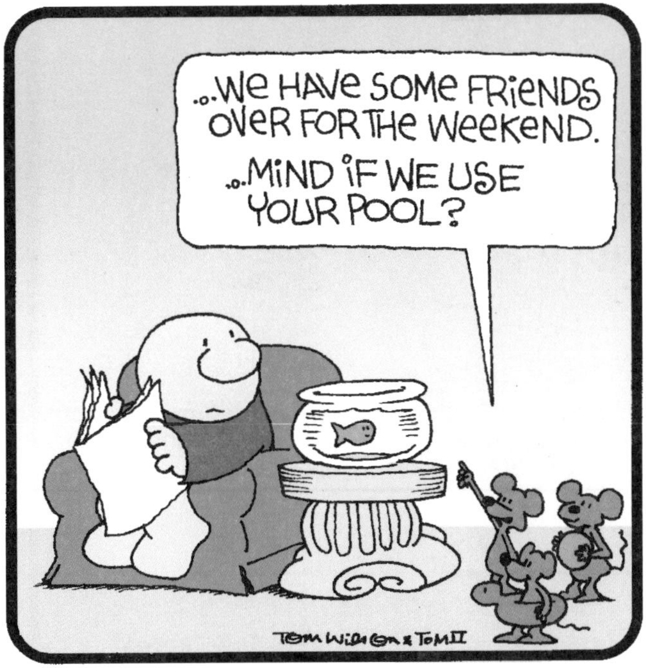
..WE HAVE SOME FRIENDS OVER FOR THE WEEKEND.
..MIND IF WE USE YOUR POOL?
Tom Wilson & Tom II

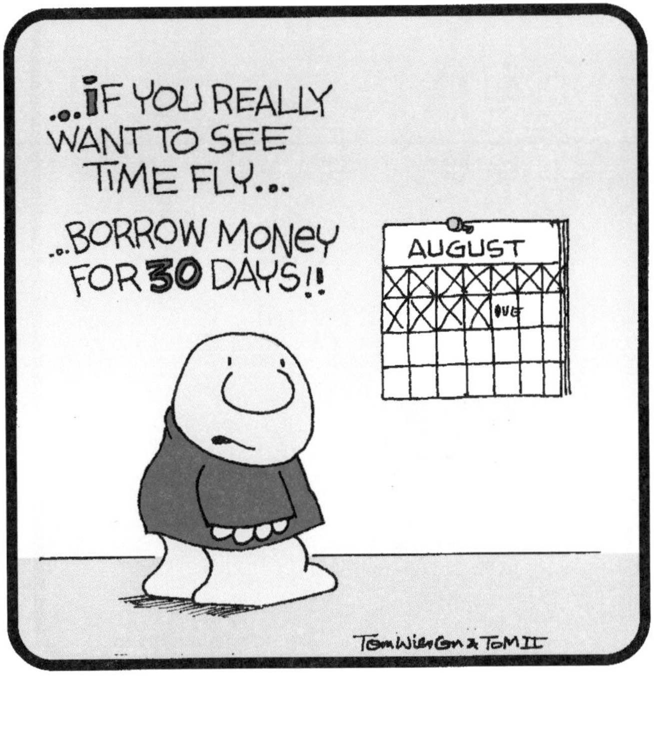
...IF YOU REALLY WANT TO SEE TIME FLY...
..BORROW MONEY FOR 30 DAYS!!
AUGUST
DUE
Tom Wilson & Tom II

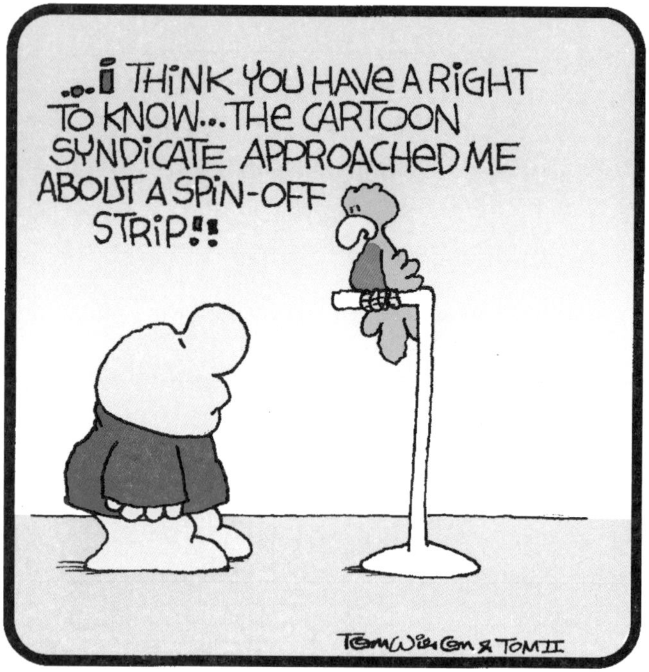
...I THINK YOU HAVE A RIGHT TO KNOW... THE CARTOON SYNDICATE APPROACHED ME ABOUT A SPIN-OFF STRIP!!
TOM WILSON & TOM II

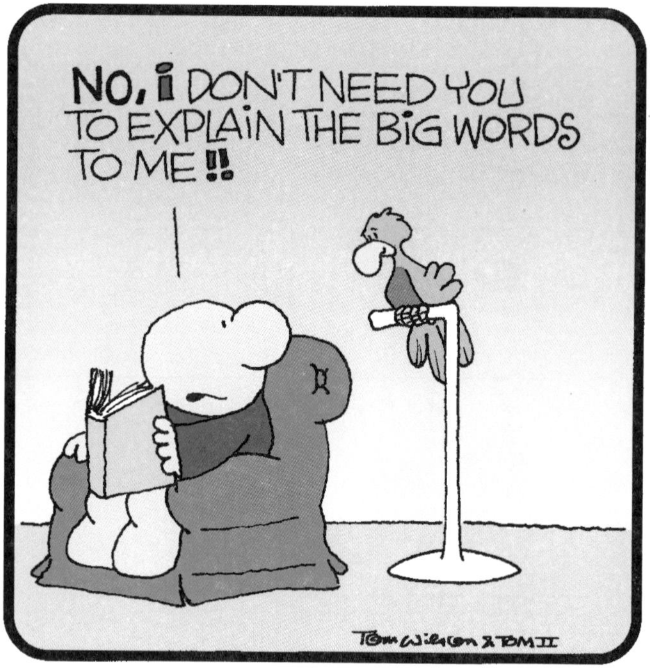
NO, I DON'T NEED YOU TO EXPLAIN THE BIG WORDS TO ME!!
TOM WILSON & TOM II

PSYCHIATRIST
PSYCHIATRIST
...IF TALK IS CHEAP, HOW COME LISTENING'S SO EXPENSIVE?!
TOM WILSON & TOM II

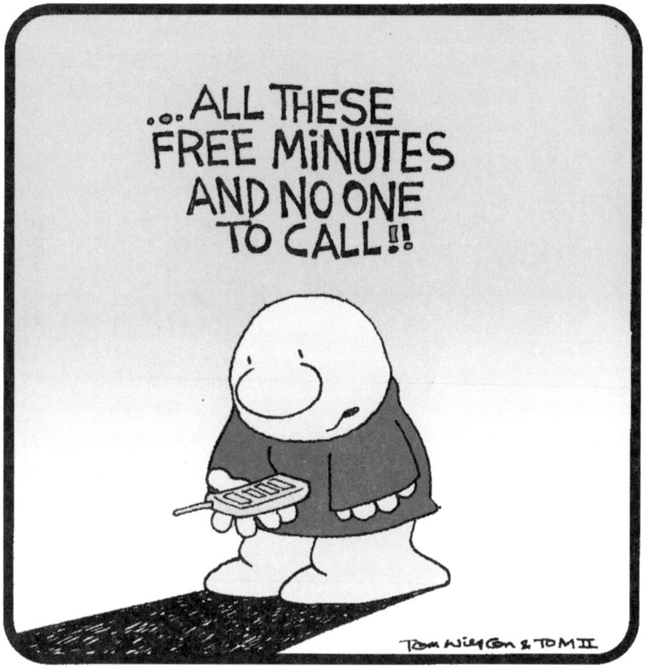
...ALL THESE FREE MINUTES AND NO ONE TO CALL!!
TOM WILSON & TOM II

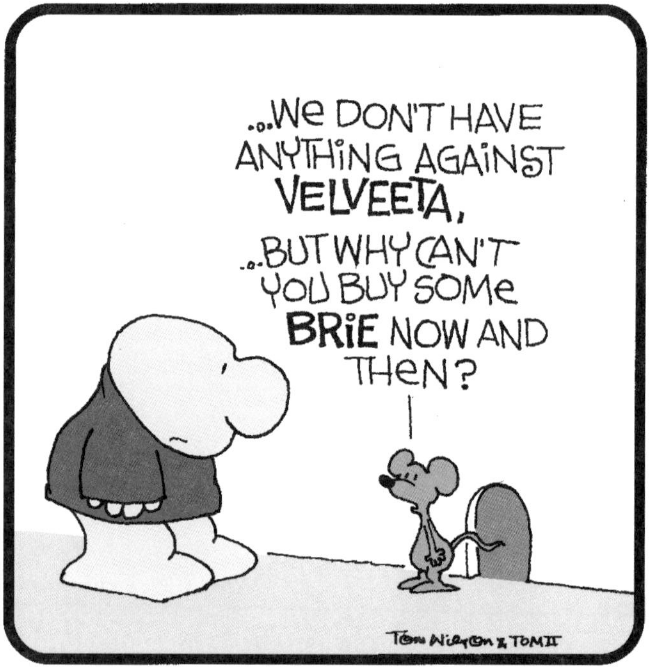
...WE DON'T HAVE ANYTHING AGAINST VELVEETA, ...BUT WHY CAN'T YOU BUY SOME BRIE NOW AND THEN?
TOM WILSON & TOM II

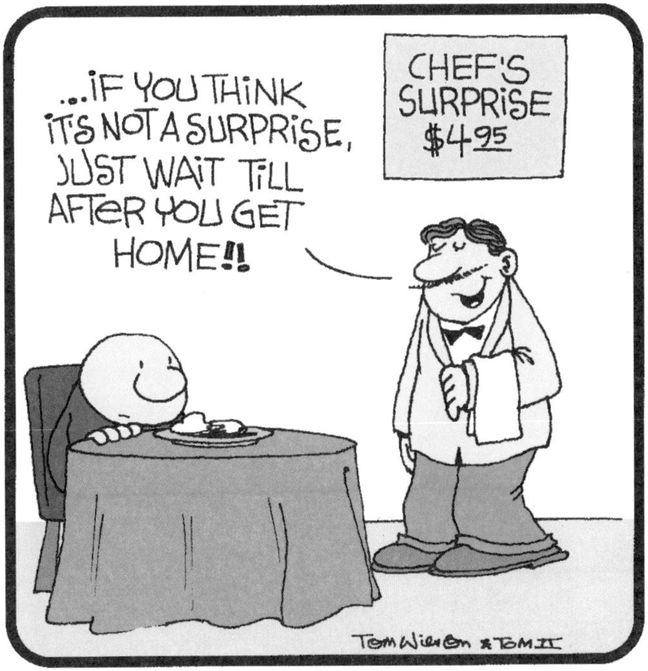
CHEF'S SURPRISE $4.95
...IF YOU THINK IT'S NOT A SURPRISE, JUST WAIT TILL AFTER YOU GET HOME!!
Tom Wilson & TOM II

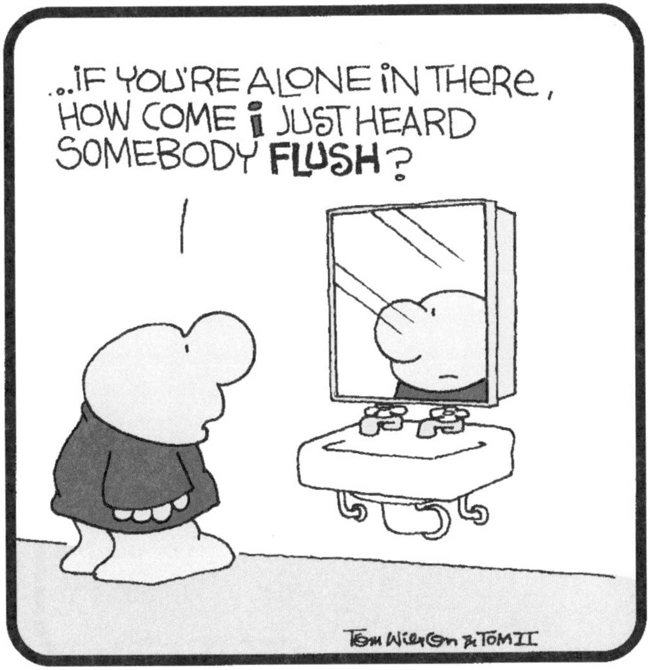
...IF YOU'RE ALONE IN THERE, HOW COME I JUST HEARD SOMEBODY FLUSH?
Tom Wilson & TOM II

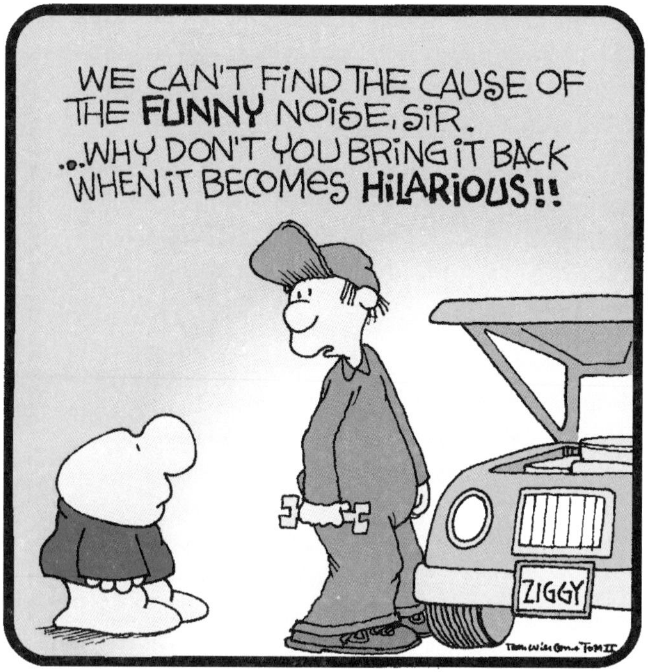
WE CAN'T FIND THE CAUSE OF THE FUNNY NOISE, SIR. ..WHY DON'T YOU BRING IT BACK WHEN IT BECOMES HILARIOUS!!
ZIGGY
Tom Wilson & Tom II

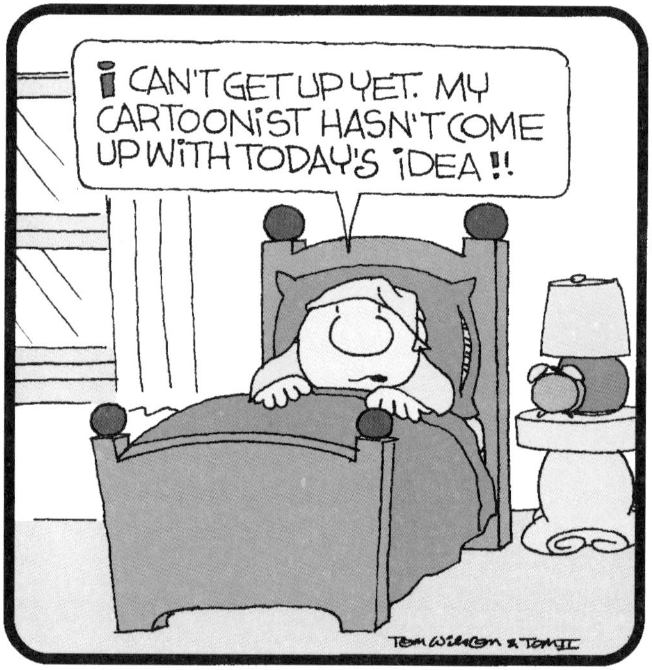
I CAN'T GET UP YET. MY CARTOONIST HASN'T COME UP WITH TODAY'S IDEA!!
Tom Wilson & Tom II

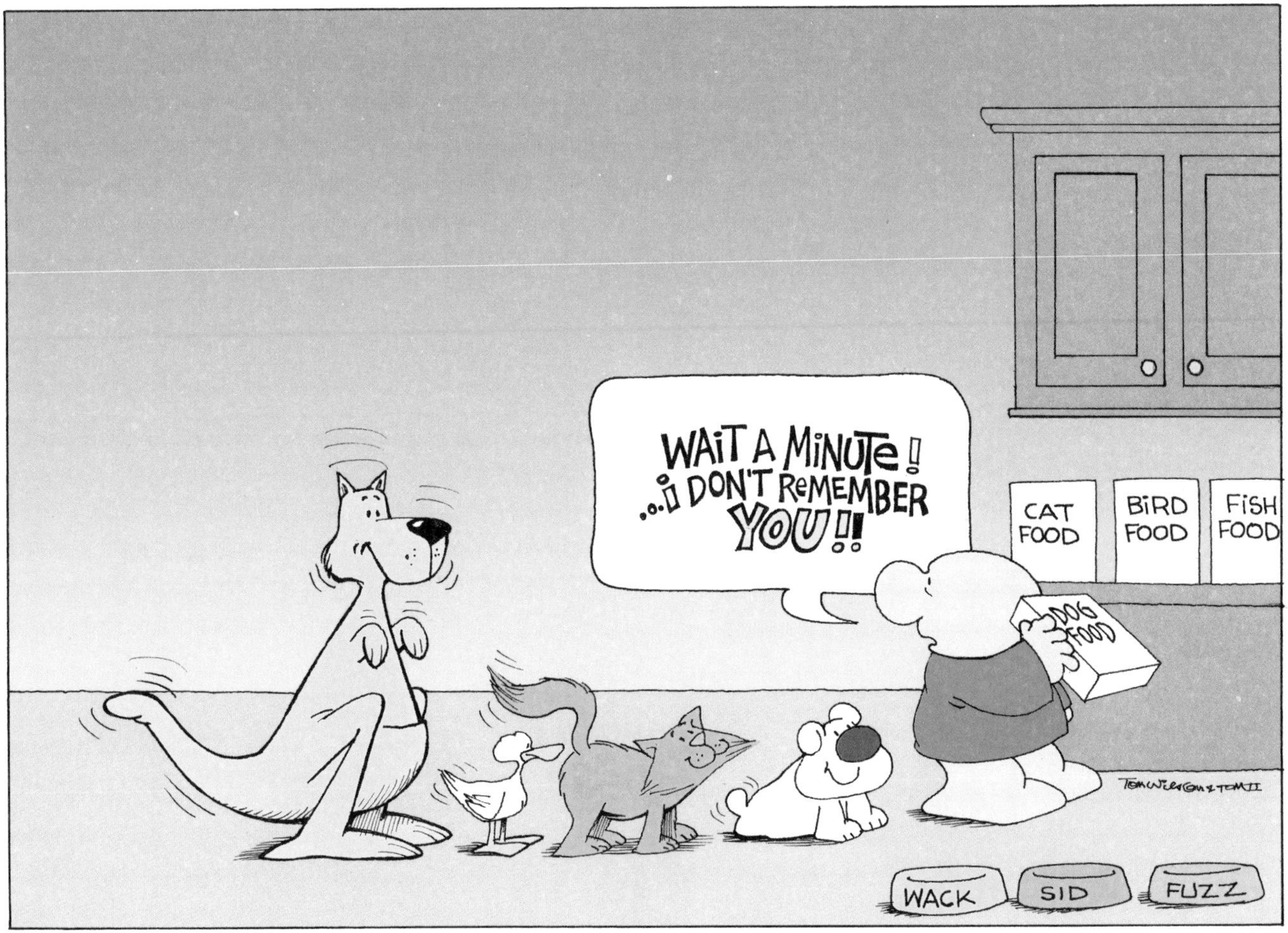
WAIT A MINUTE!
...I DON'T REMEMBER
YOU!!
CAT FOOD
BIRD FOOD
FISH FOOD
DOG FOOD
WACK
SID
FUZZ

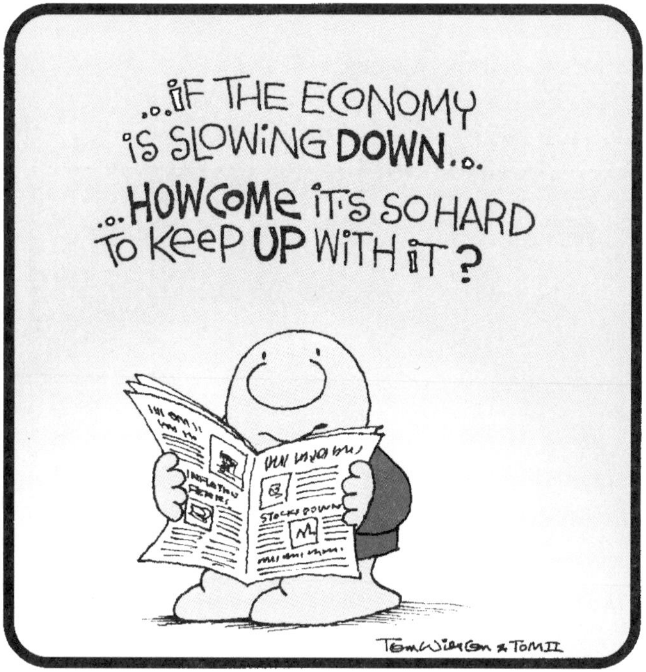
...IF THE ECONOMY IS SLOWING DOWN...
...HOW COME IT'S SO HARD TO KEEP UP WITH IT?
STOCKS DOWN
TOM WILSON & TOM II

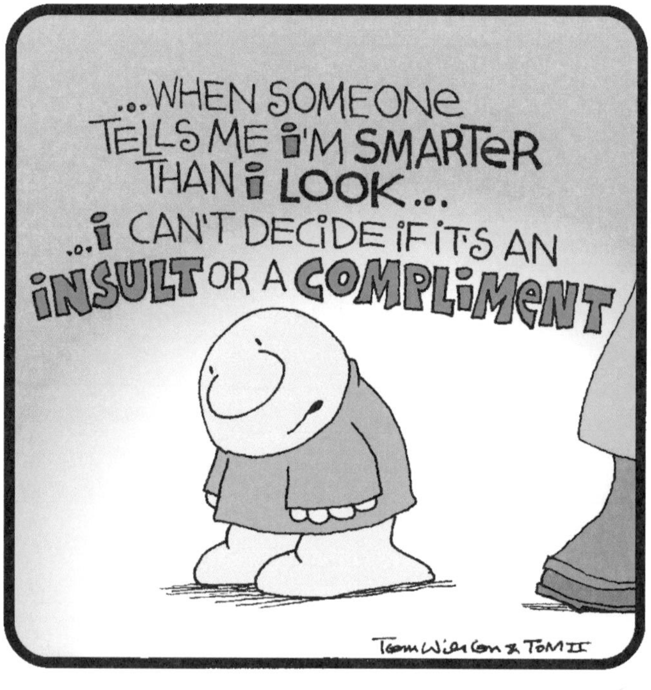
...WHEN SOMEONE TELLS ME I'M SMARTER THAN I LOOK...
...I CAN'T DECIDE IF IT'S AN INSULT OR A COMPLIMENT
TOM WILSON & TOM II

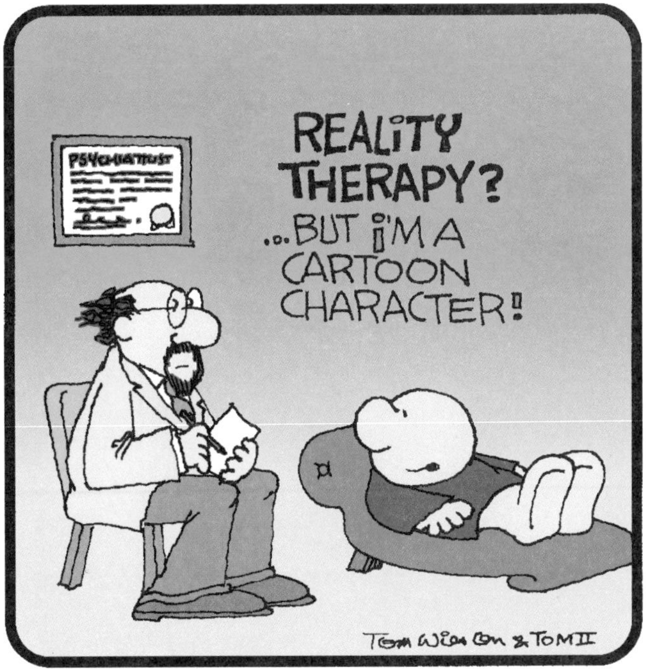
PSYCHIATRIST
REALITY THERAPY? ...BUT I'M A CARTOON CHARACTER!
TOM WILSON & TOM II

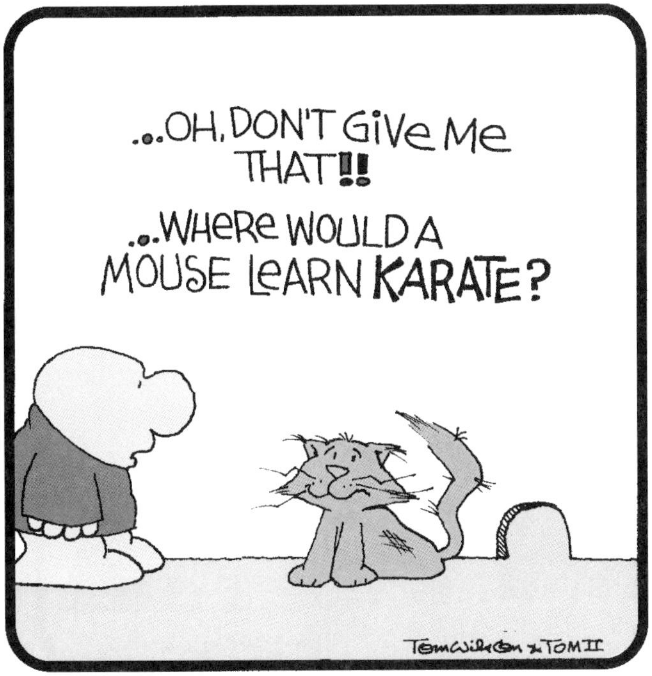
...OH, DON'T GIVE ME THAT!!
...WHERE WOULD A MOUSE LEARN KARATE?
TOM WILSON & TOM II

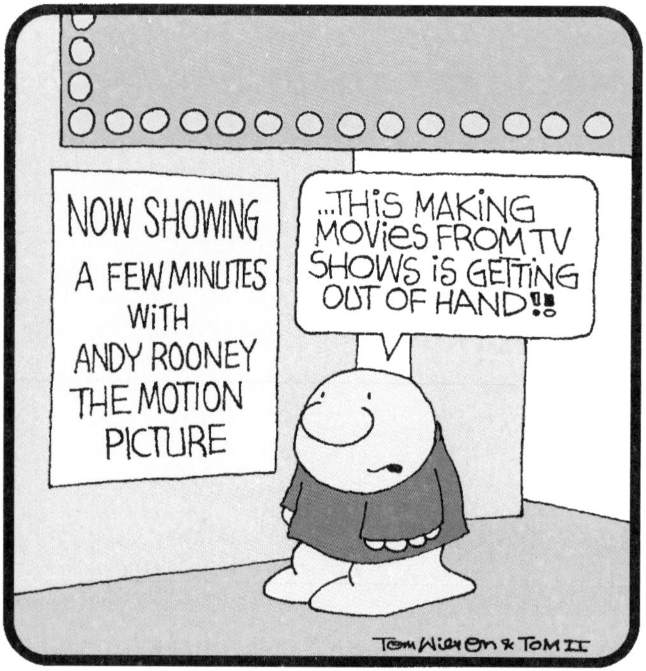
NOW SHOWING
A FEW MINUTES
WITH
ANDY ROONEY
THE MOTION
PICTURE
...THIS MAKING MOVIES FROM TV SHOWS IS GETTING OUT OF HAND!!
TOM WILSON & TOM II

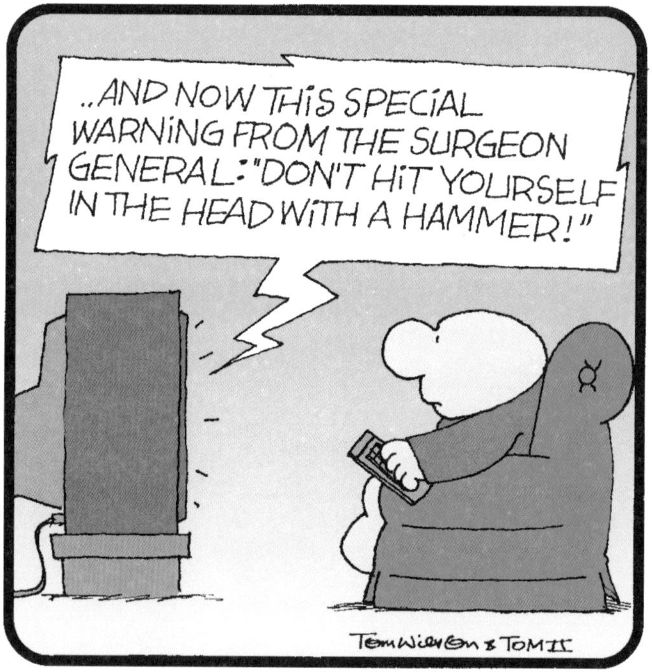
..AND NOW THIS SPECIAL WARNING FROM THE SURGEON GENERAL: "DON'T HIT YOURSELF IN THE HEAD WITH A HAMMER!"
TOM WILSON & TOM II

MADAME CLEO KNOWS ALL. CALL THE PSYCHIC BUDDIES HOTLINE FOR YOUR PSYCHIC READING TODAY!
WELCOME TO THE PSYCHIC BUDDIES NETWORK... IT'S FOUR DOLLARS PER MINUTE. PLEASE **HOLD**!!
THIS IS MADAME CLEO... PLEASE **WAIT** WHILE I GET IN TOUCH WITH THE SPIRIT WORLD!
...ER OKAY!
OH...YEAH! I'M GETTING IN TOUCH WITH THEM NOW... THE SPIRITS HAVE A VERY IMPORTANT MESSAGE FOR YOU... PLEASE WAIT WHILE I CONSULT FURTHER.
?
...THE SPIRITS TELL ME THAT THIS IS A TIME OF GREAT GROWTH FOR YOU... PLEASE **HOLD** WHILE I GET DEEPER INTO MY TRANCE!
?
OOOO..AHHH ..OHHHHHH...WOOOOOU
...I DON'T KNOW ABOUT **ME**, BUT THIS IS CERTAINLY A TIME OF **GREAT GROWTH** FOR MY **PHONE BILL**!!
NOOOOOOOOOAHHHH

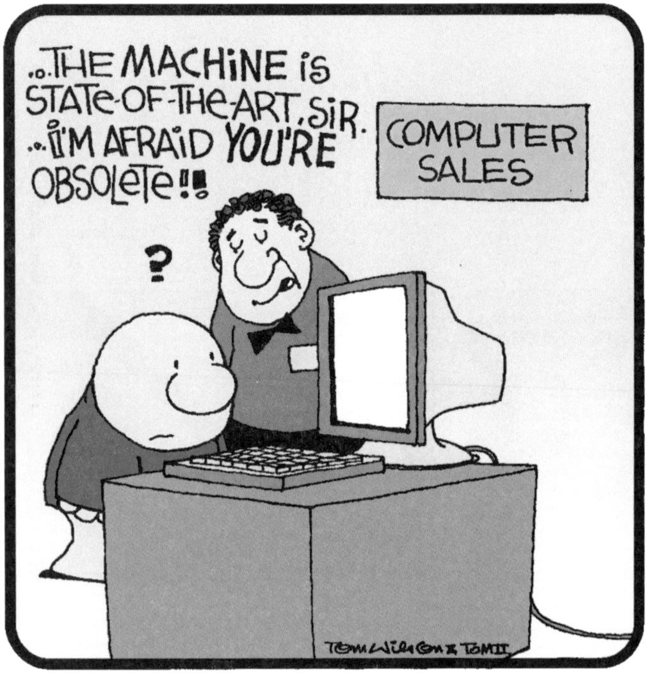
..THE MACHINE IS STATE-OF-THE-ART, SIR. ..I'M AFRAID YOU'RE OBSOLETE!!
COMPUTER SALES
?
TOM WILSON & TOM II

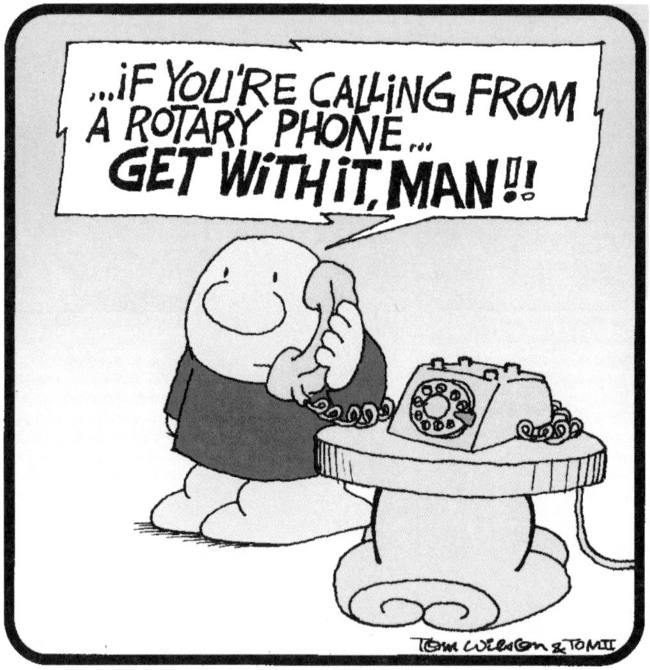
...IF YOU'RE CALLING FROM A ROTARY PHONE... GET WITH IT, MAN!!
TOM WILSON & TOM II

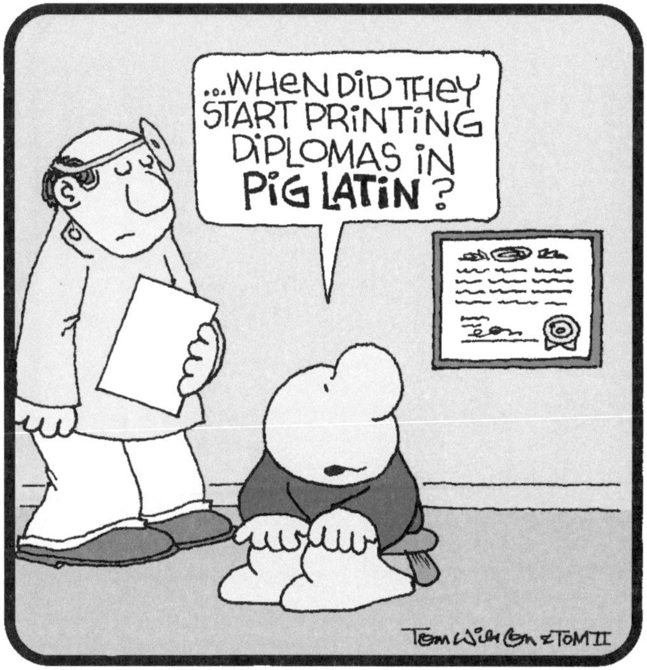
...WHEN DID THEY START PRINTING DIPLOMAS IN PIG LATIN?
Tom Wilson & TOM II

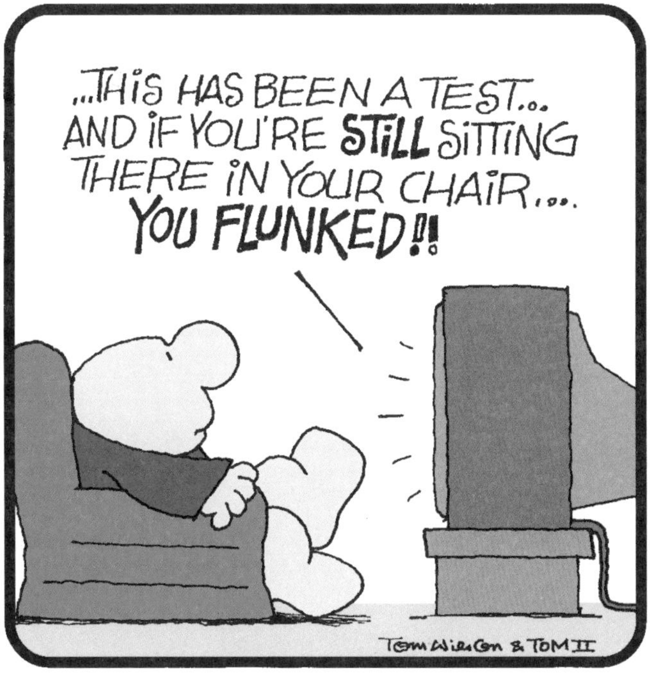
...THIS HAS BEEN A TEST... AND IF YOU'RE STILL SITTING THERE IN YOUR CHAIR.... YOU FLUNKED!!
Tom Wilson & TOM II

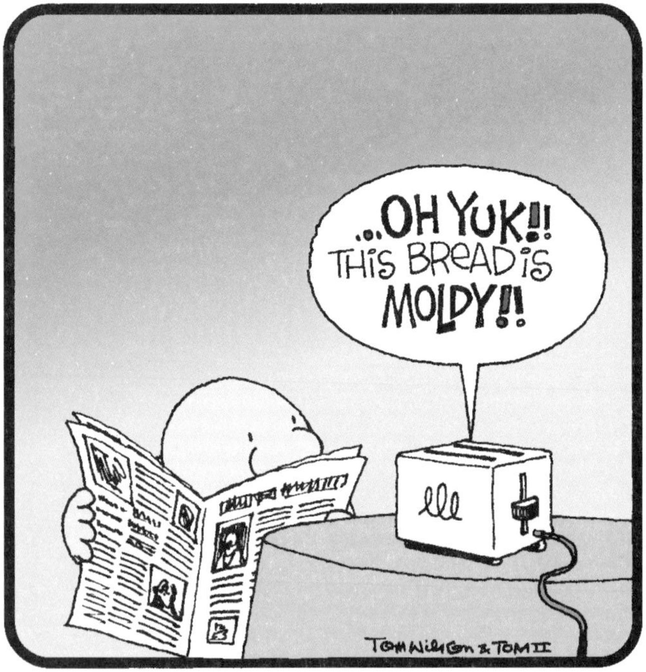
...OH YUK!! THIS BREAD IS MOLDY!!
TOM WILSON & TOM II

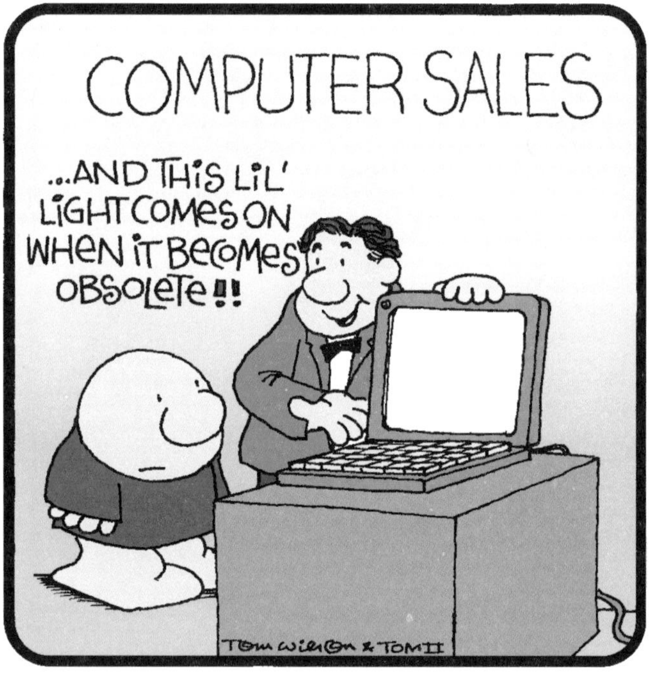
COMPUTER SALES
...AND THIS LIL' LIGHT COMES ON WHEN IT BECOMES OBSOLETE!!
TOM WILSON & TOM II

...I THINK I'M IN A RUT, JOSH!!
...EVERY DAY SEEMS LIKE A RERUN OF THE DAY BEFORE.
..AND THE ONLY RELIEF I GET FROM MY DAILY ROUTINES ARE MY WEEKLY ROUTINES!!
...WELL, I HEREBY RESOLVE TO DO SOMETHING ABOUT IT!!
...STARTING TOMORROW I'M GOING TO DO SOMETHING NEW AND SPONTANEOUS EVERY DAY!!
...THAT WOULD BE VERY INSPIRING IF HE DIDN'T GIVE THAT SAME SPEECH AT LEAST ONCE A WEEK!!

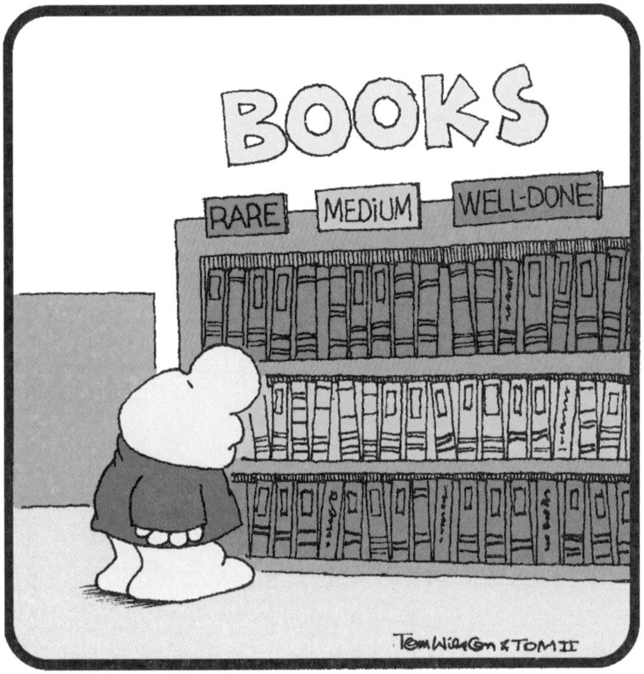
BOOKS
RARE
MEDIUM
WELL-DONE

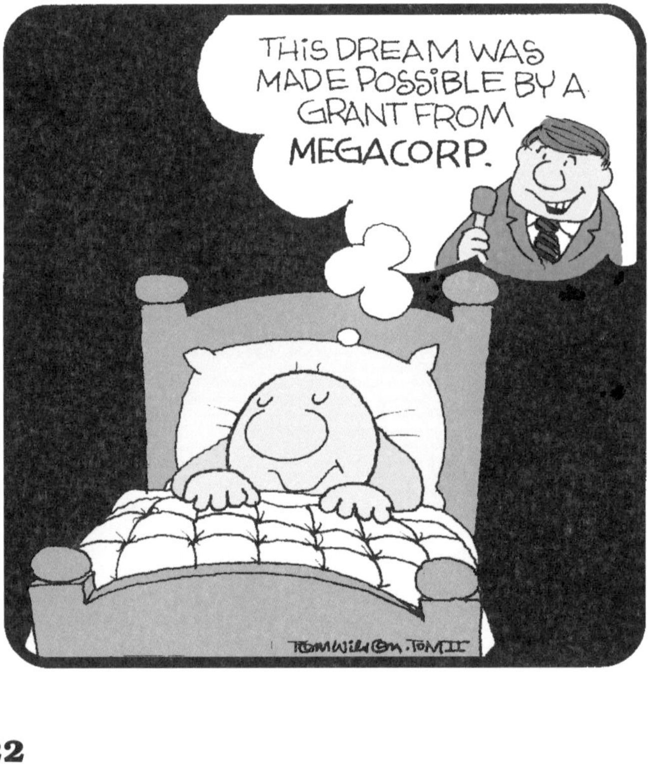
THIS DREAM WAS MADE POSSIBLE BY A GRANT FROM MEGACORP.

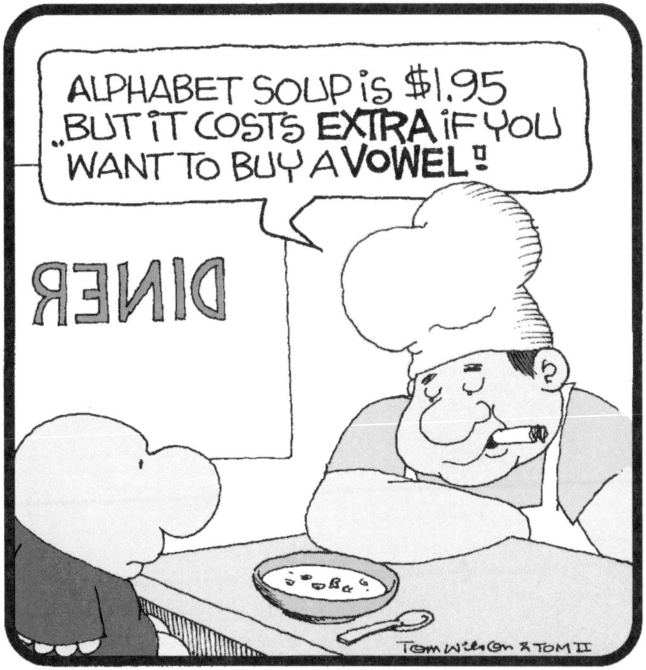
ALPHABET SOUP is $1.95 ..BUT iT COSTS EXTRA iF YOU WANT TO BUY A VOWEL!
DINER
Tom Wilson & TOM II

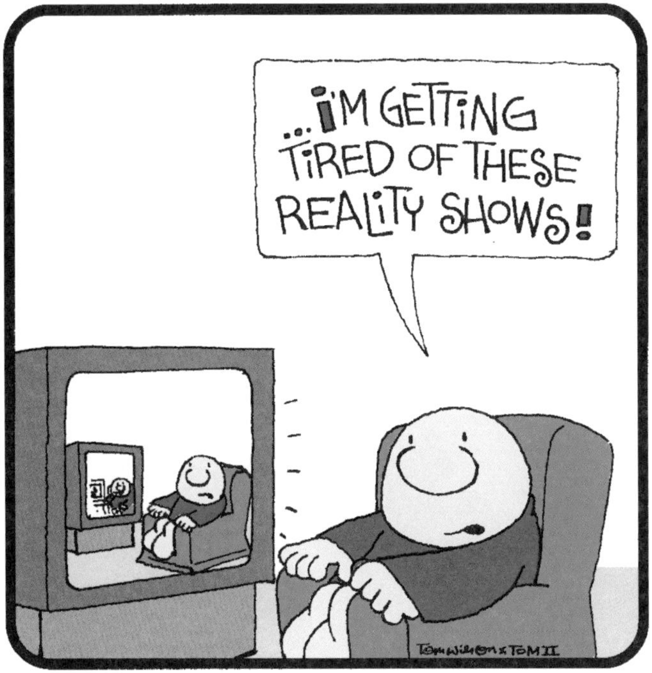
...i'M GETTiNG TiRED OF THESE REALiTY SHOWS!
Tom Wilson & TOM II

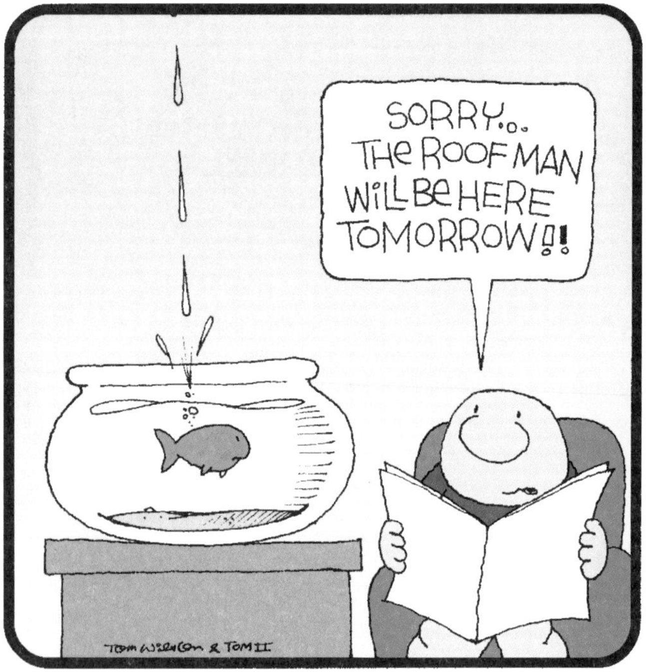
SORRY... THE ROOF MAN WILL BE HERE TOMORROW!!
TOM WILSON & TOM II

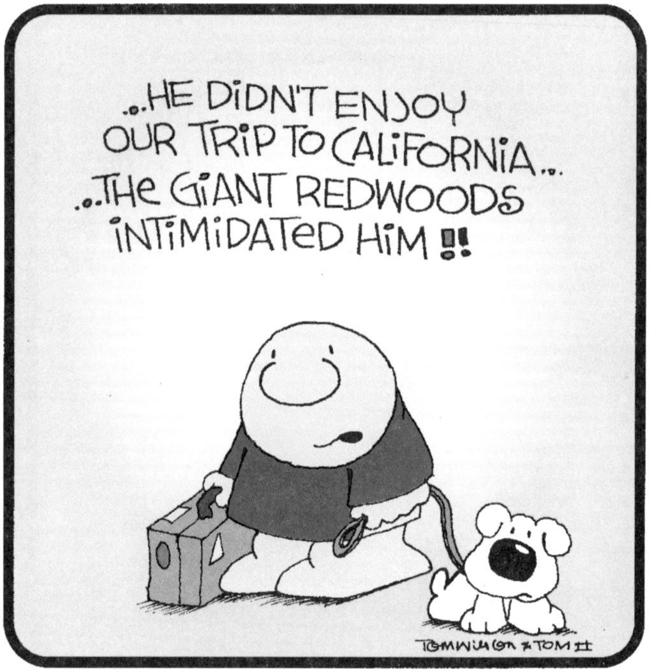
...HE DIDN'T ENJOY OUR TRIP TO CALIFORNIA... ...THE GIANT REDWOODS INTIMIDATED HIM!!
TOM WILSON & TOM II

NEXT WINDOW
NEXT WINDOW
NEXT WINDOW
NEXT WINDOW
NEXT WINDOW
NEXT WINDOW
NEXT WINDOW
NEXT WINDOW
NEXT BUILDING
TOM WILSON & TOM II

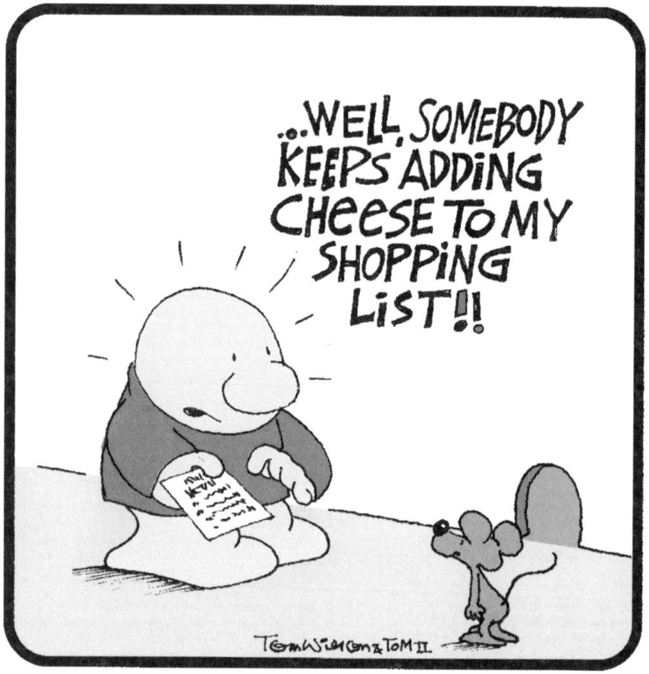
..WELL, SOMEBODY KEEPS ADDING CHEESE TO MY SHOPPING LIST!!
Tom Wilson & Tom II

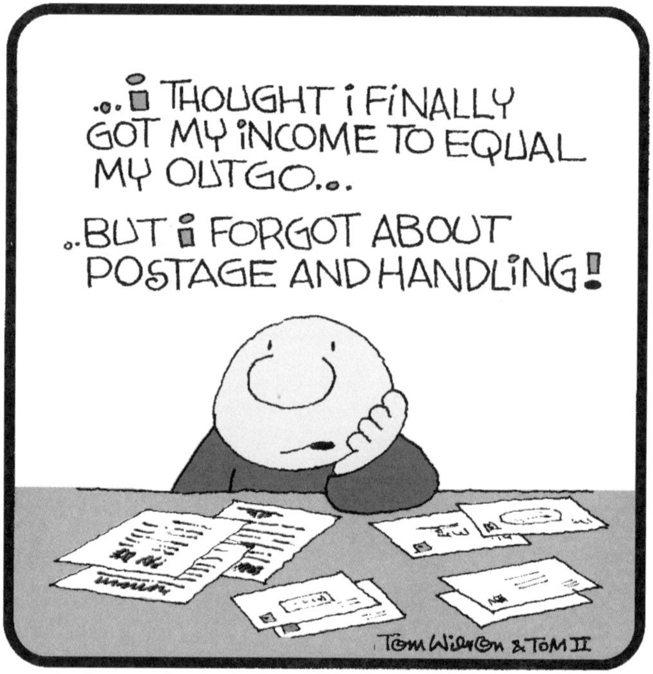
..I THOUGHT I FINALLY GOT MY INCOME TO EQUAL MY OUTGO...
..BUT I FORGOT ABOUT POSTAGE AND HANDLING!
Tom Wilson & Tom II

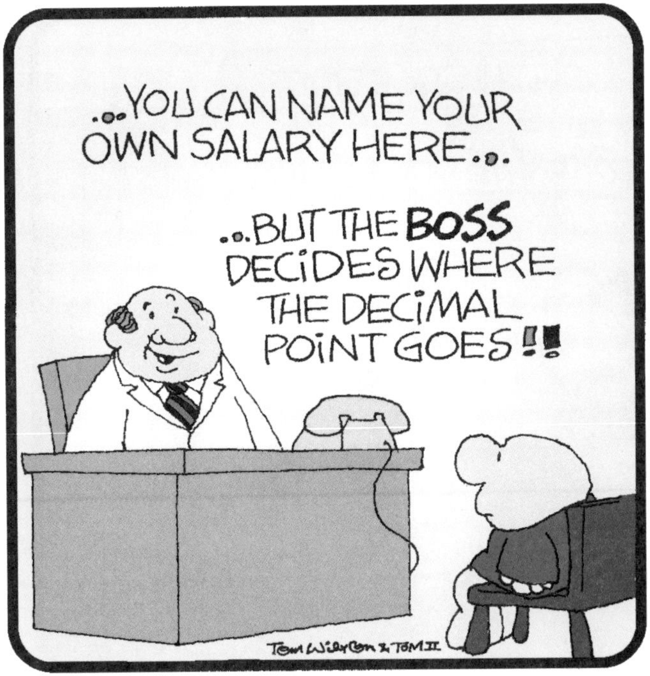
...YOU CAN NAME YOUR OWN SALARY HERE...
...BUT THE BOSS DECIDES WHERE THE DECIMAL POINT GOES!!
Tom Wilson & Tom II

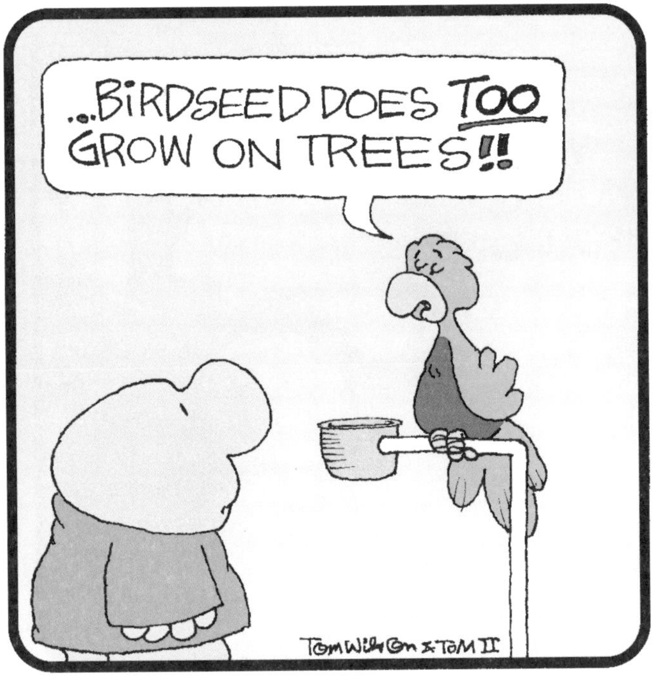
...BIRDSEED DOES TOO GROW ON TREES!!
Tom Wilson & Tom II

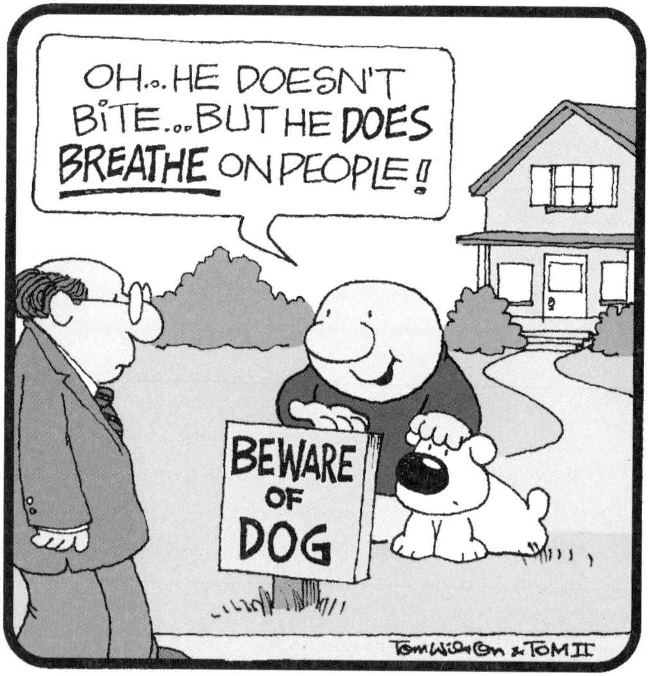
OH... HE DOESN'T BITE... BUT HE DOES BREATHE ON PEOPLE!!
BEWARE OF DOG
Tom Wilson & TOM II

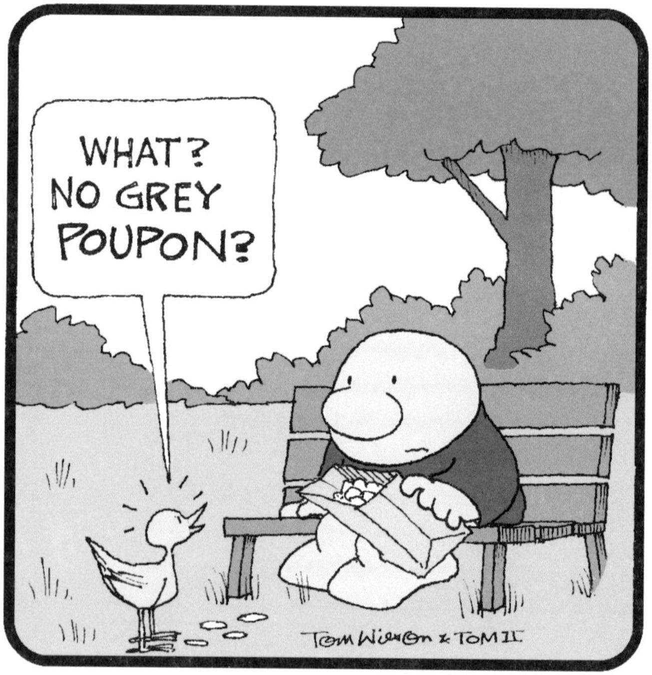
WHAT? NO GREY POUPON?
Tom Wilson & TOM II

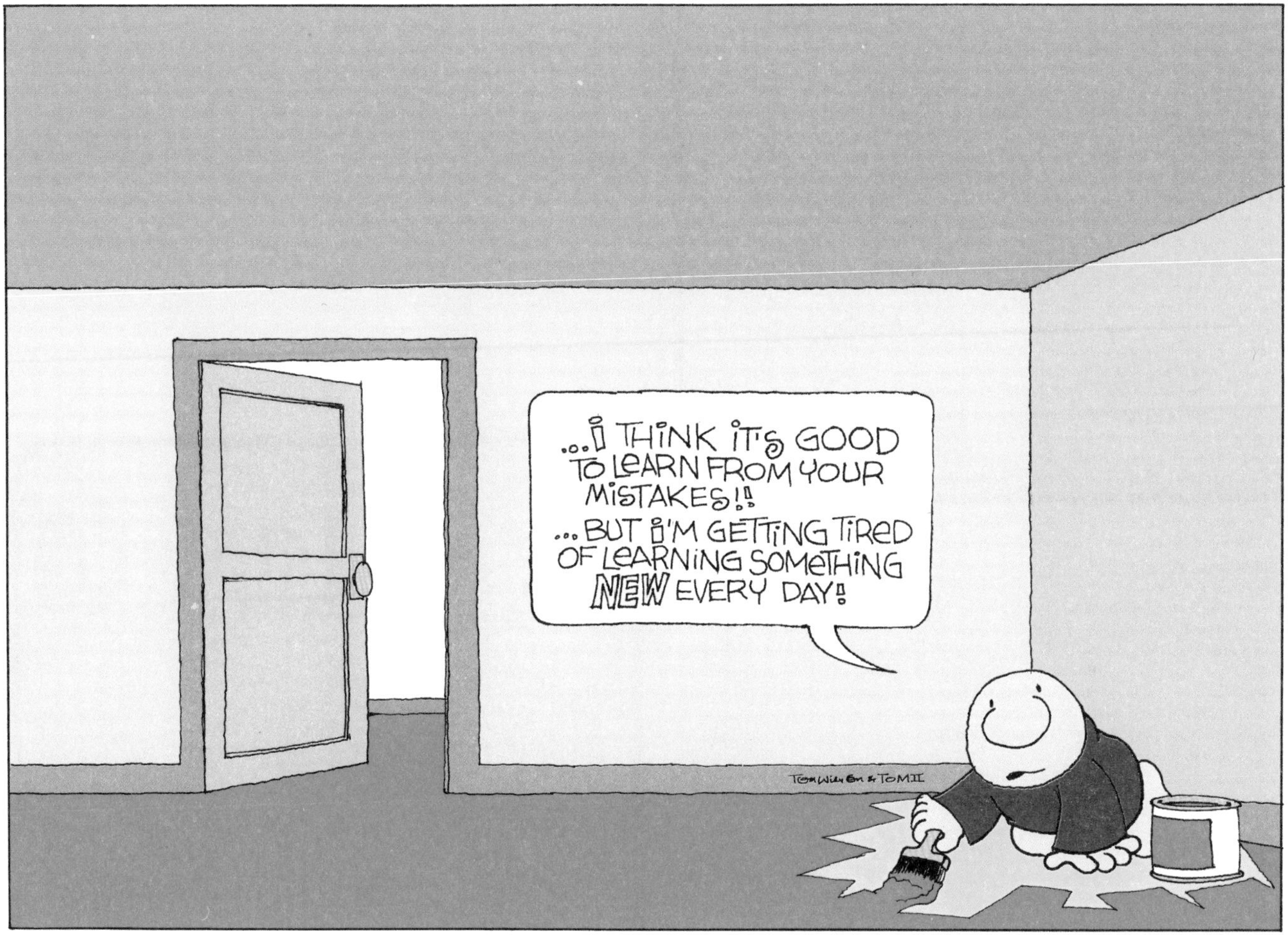
...I THINK IT'S GOOD TO LEARN FROM YOUR MISTAKES!!
...BUT I'M GETTING TIRED OF LEARNING SOMETHING NEW EVERY DAY!
TOM WILSON & TOM II

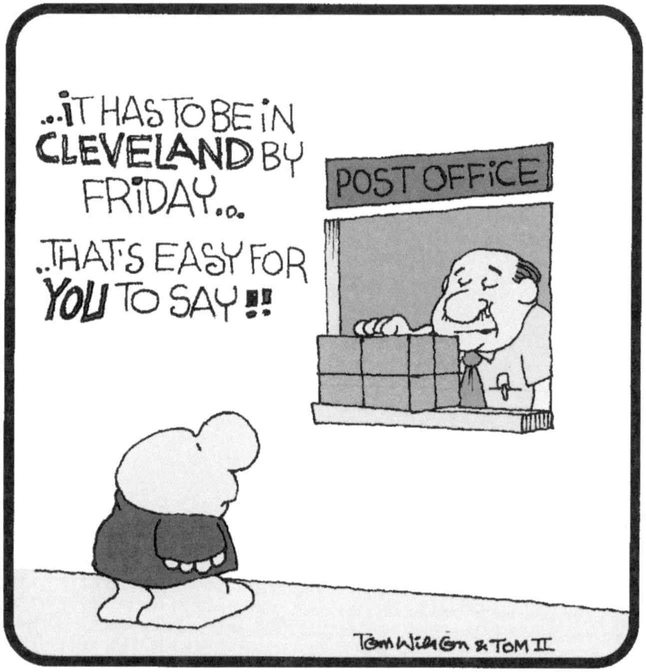
..iT HAS TO BE iN CLEVELAND BY FRiDAY...
..THAT'S EASY FOR YOU TO SAY!!
POST OFFiCE
TomWilson & TOM II

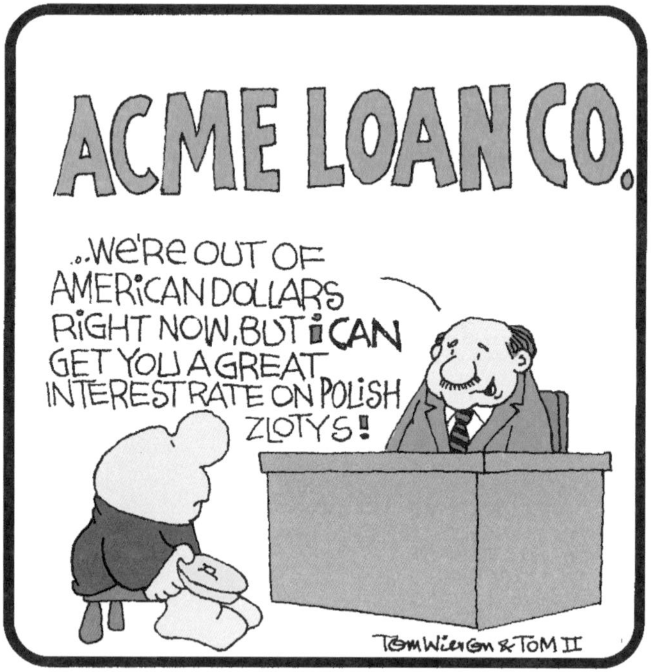
ACME LOAN CO.
..We're OUT OF AMERiCAN DOLLARS RiGHT NOW, BUT i CAN GET YOU A GREAT INTEREST RATE ON POLiSH ZLOTYS!
TomWilson & TOM II

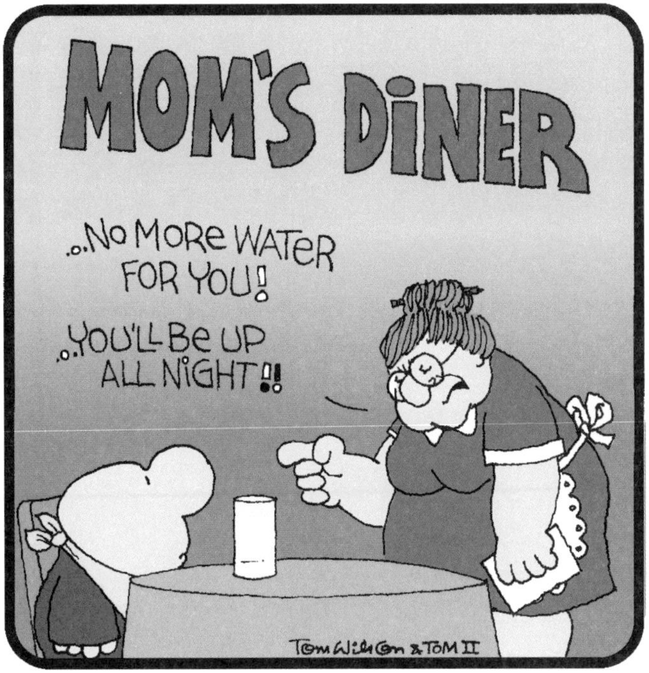
MOM'S DiNER
..No MORE WATER FOR YOU!
..YOU'LL Be UP ALL NiGHT!!
Tom Wilson & TOM II

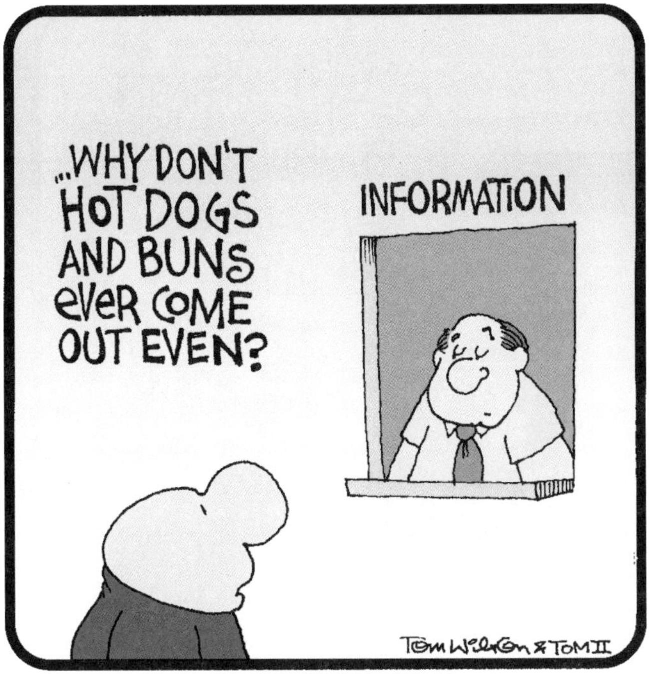
...WHY DON'T HOT DOGS AND BUNS ever COME OUT EVEN?
INFORMATION
Tom Wilson & TOM II

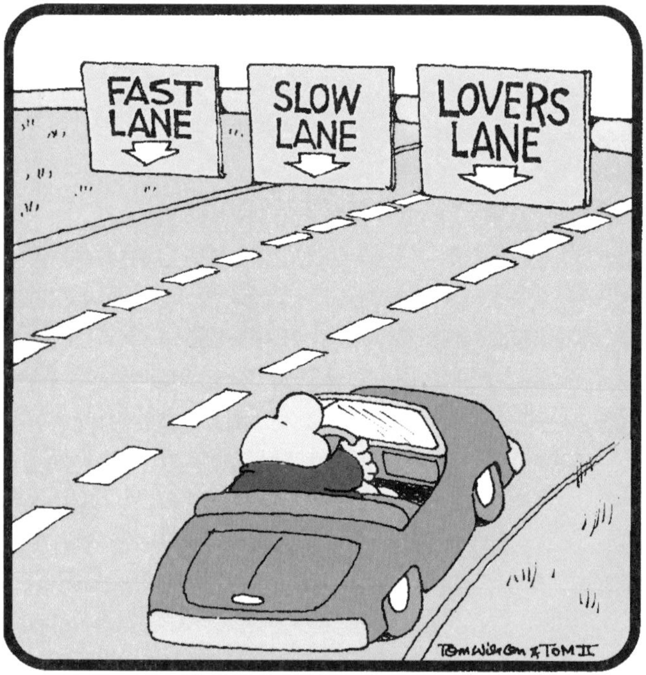
FAST LANE
SLOW LANE
LOVERS LANE
Tom Wilson & Tom II

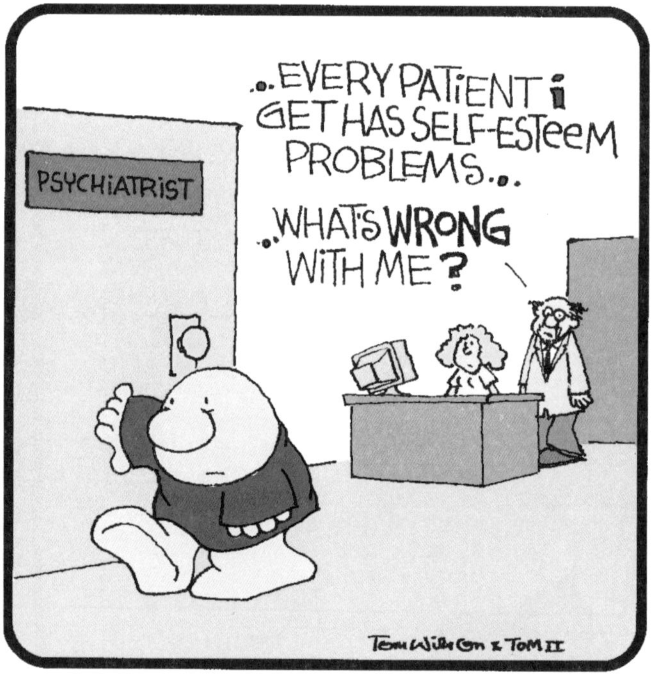
..EVERY PATIENT i GET HAS SELF-ESTEEM PROBLEMS...
..WHAT'S WRONG WITH ME?
PSYCHIATRIST
Tom Wilson & Tom II

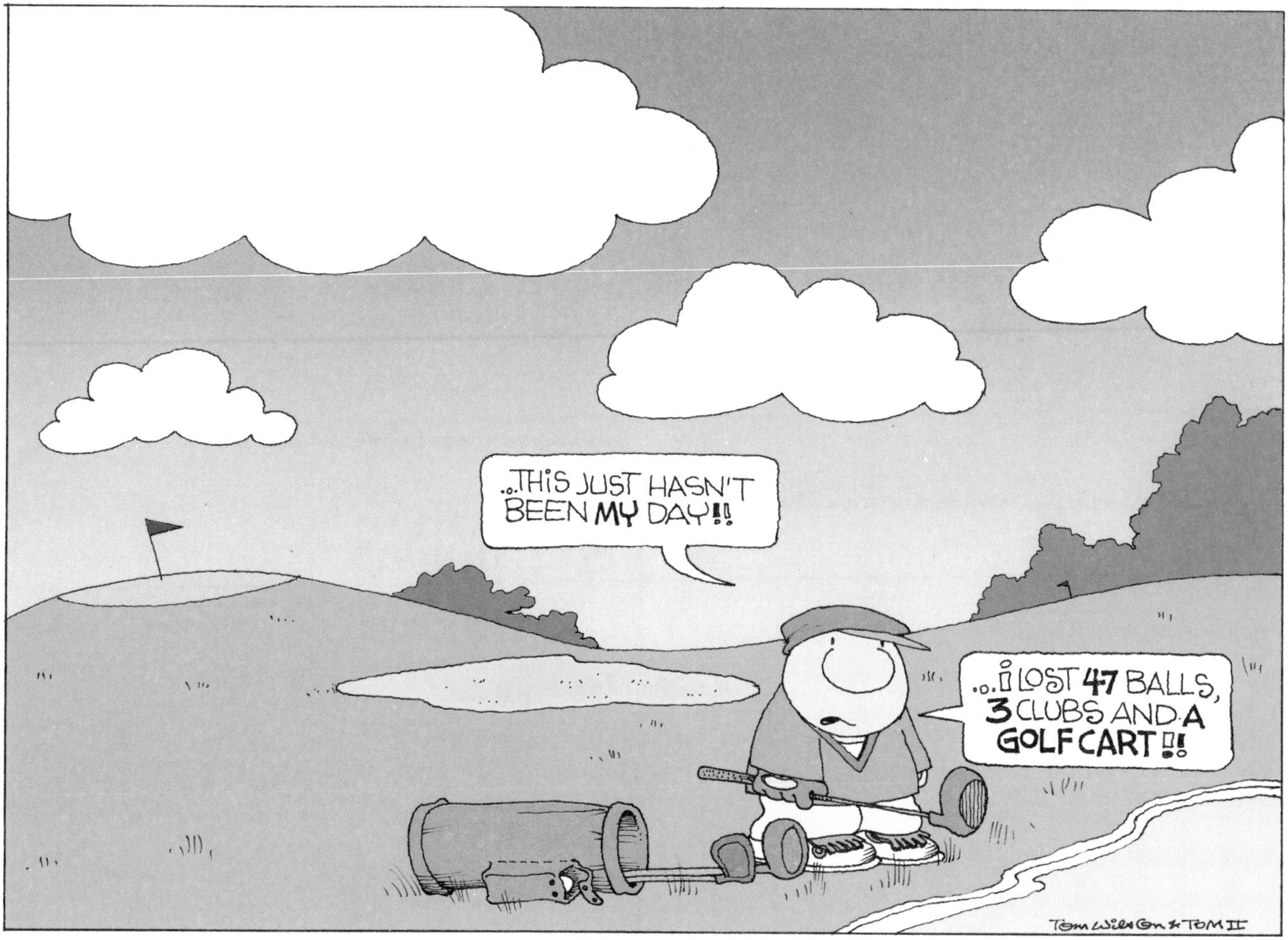
..THIS JUST HASN'T BEEN MY DAY!!
..o..I LOST 47 BALLS, 3 CLUBS AND A GOLF CART!!
Tom Wilson & TOM II

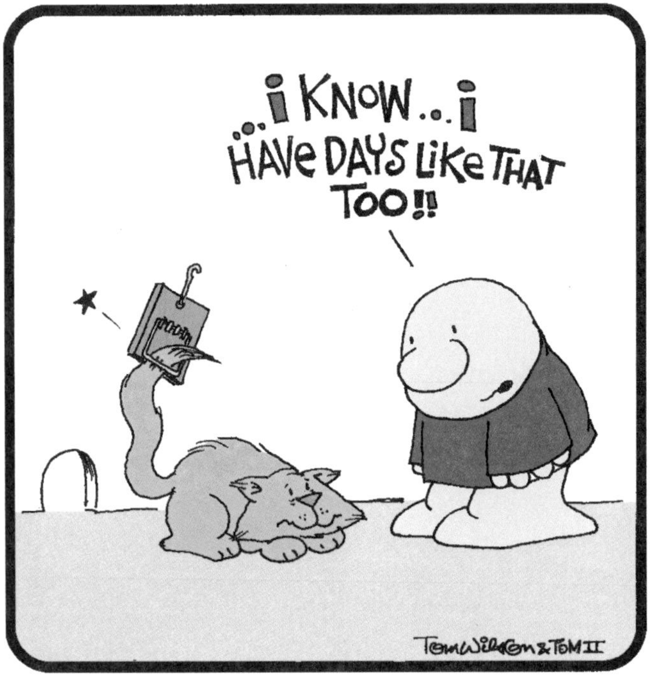
...i KNOW...i HAVE DAYS LIKE THAT TOO!!
TomWilson&TOM II

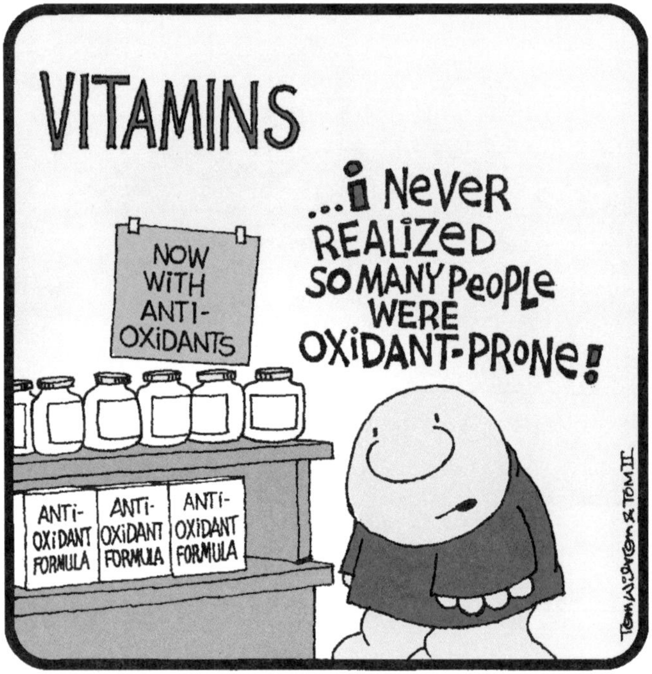
VITAMINS
NOW WITH ANTI-OXIDANTS
ANTI-OXIDANT FORMULA
ANTI-OXIDANT FORMULA
ANTI-OXIDANT FORMULA
...i NEVER REALIZED SO MANY PEOPLE WERE OXIDANT-PRONE!
TomWilson&TOM II

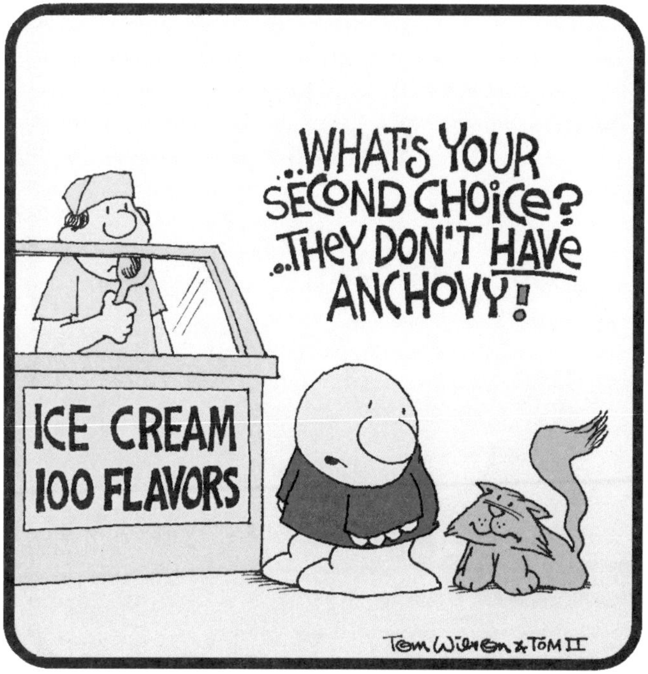
..WHAT'S YOUR SECOND CHOICE? ..THEY DON'T HAVE ANCHOVY!
ICE CREAM 100 FLAVORS
Tom Wilson & Tom II

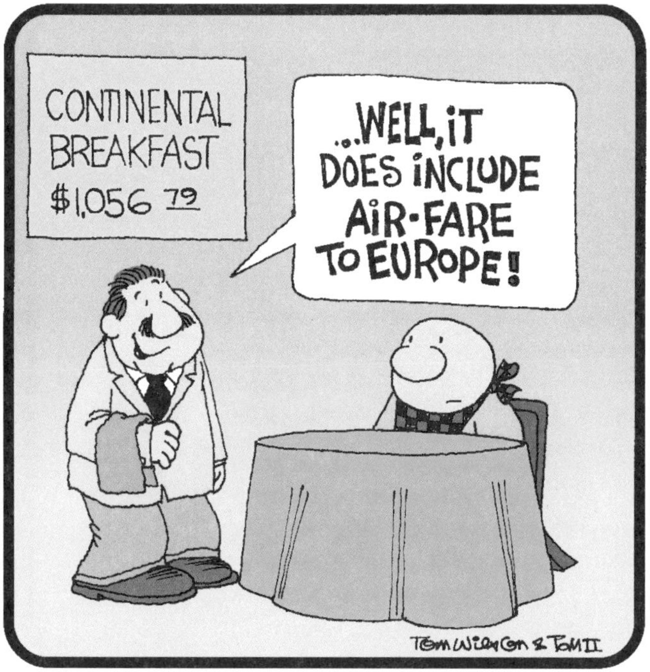
CONTINENTAL BREAKFAST $1,056 79
...WELL, IT DOES INCLUDE AIR-FARE TO EUROPE!
Tom Wilson & Tom II

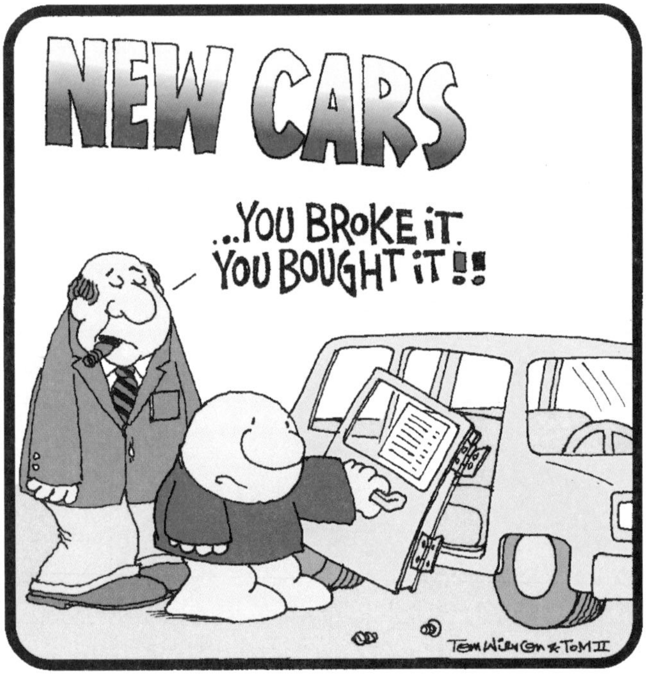
NEW CARS
...YOU BROKE iT YOU BOUGHT iT!!
TOM WILSON & TOM II

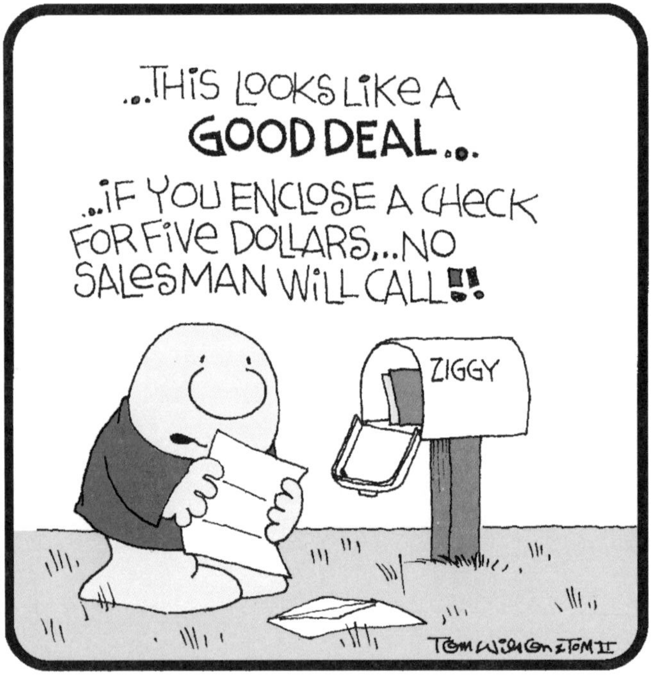
...THIS LOOKS LIKE A GOOD DEAL...
...iF YOU ENCLOSE A CHECK FOR FIVE DOLLARS,...NO SALESMAN WILL CALL!!
ZIGGY
TOM WILSON & TOM II

...STAY TUNED FOR "GOTTA SWEAT"!
...ALL RIGHT PEOPLE, IT'S TIME FOR LEG LIFTS! ONE-AND-TWO ONE-AND-TWO ONE-AND-TWO NOW THE OTHER LEG...
LIFT HIGHER... HIGHER... HIGHER
..HIGHER... C'MON PEOPLE.. LIFT UP THOSE LEGS...
ZIP
...FOR ME... EXERCISE IS MORE A CASE OF ERROBICS!!
TOM WILSON & TOM II

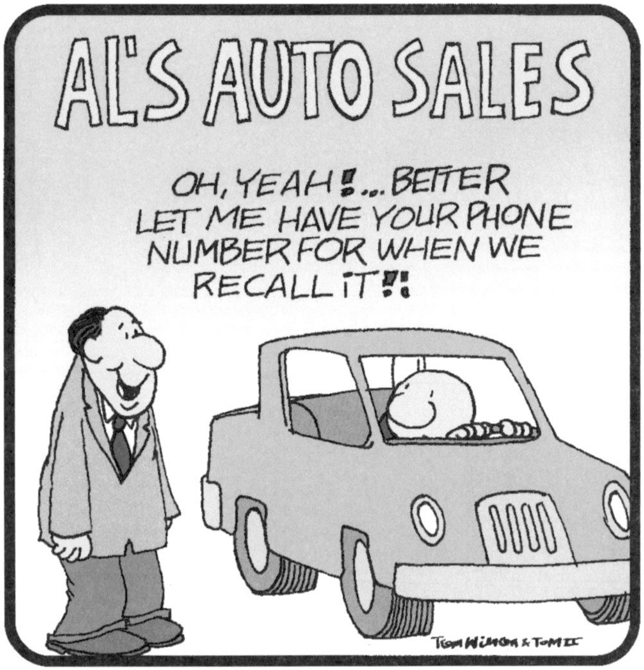
AL'S AUTO SALES
OH, YEAH!...BETTER LET ME HAVE YOUR PHONE NUMBER FOR WHEN WE RECALL IT!!

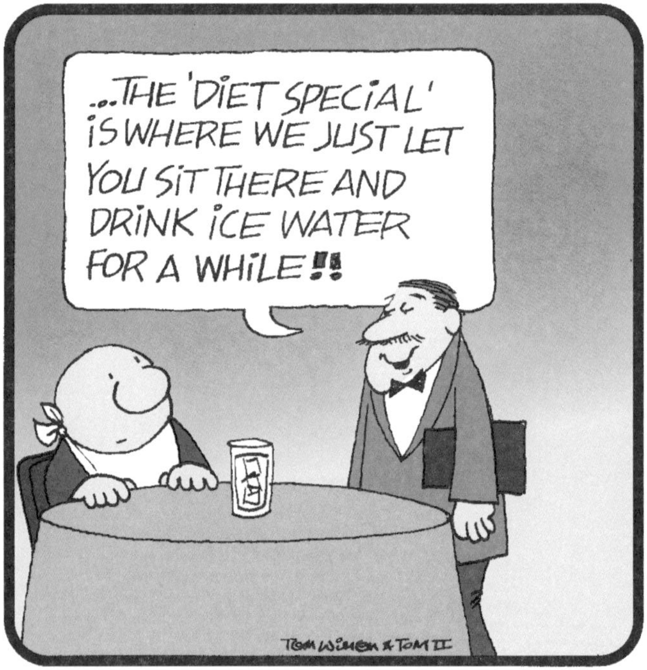
...THE 'DIET SPECIAL' IS WHERE WE JUST LET YOU SIT THERE AND DRINK ICE WATER FOR A WHILE!!

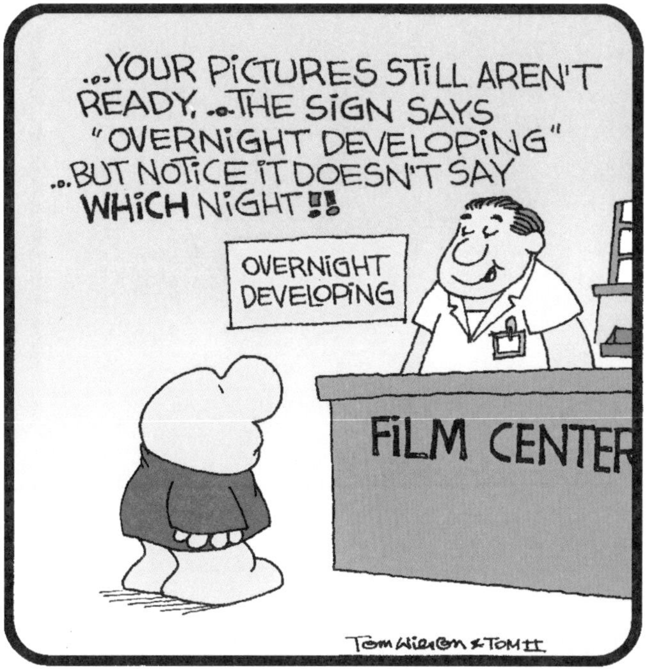
...YOUR PICTURES STILL AREN'T READY, ..THE SIGN SAYS "OVERNIGHT DEVELOPING" ...BUT NOTICE IT DOESN'T SAY **WHICH** NIGHT!!
OVERNIGHT DEVELOPING
FILM CENTER
TOM WILSON & TOM II

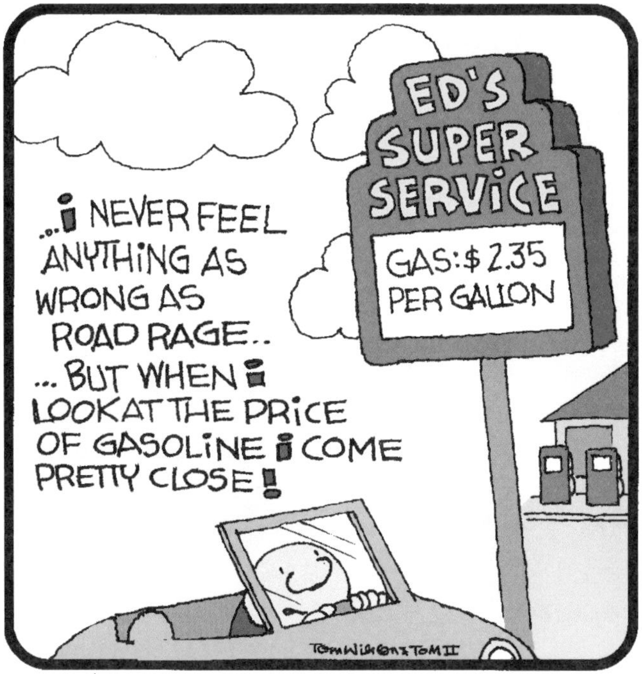
ED'S SUPER SERVICE
GAS: $2.35 PER GALLON
...I NEVER FEEL ANYTHING AS WRONG AS ROAD RAGE.. ...BUT WHEN I LOOK AT THE PRICE OF GASOLINE I COME PRETTY CLOSE!
TOM WILSON & TOM II

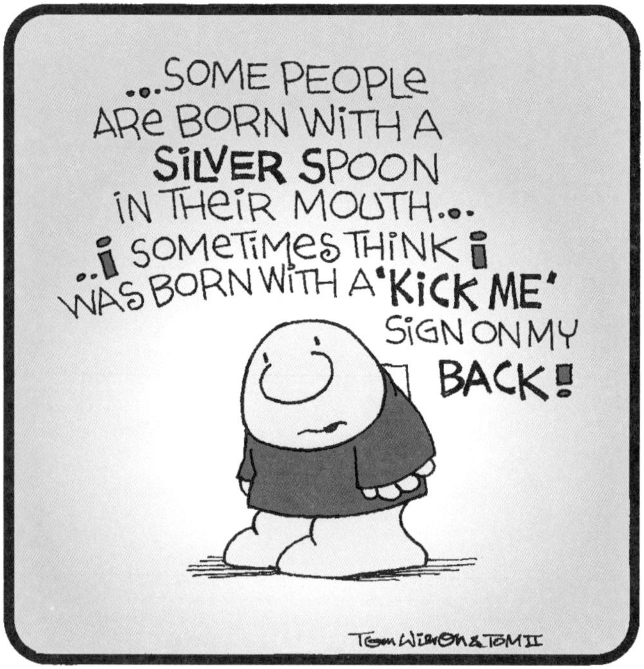
...SOME PEOPLE ARE BORN WITH A SILVER SPOON IN THEIR MOUTH... ..I SOMETIMES THINK I WAS BORN WITH A 'KICK ME' SIGN ON MY BACK!
TOM WILSON & TOM II

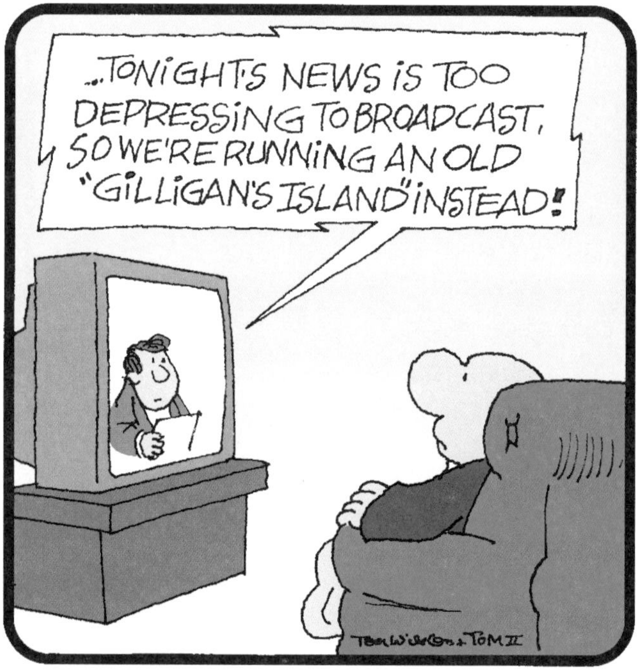
..TONIGHT'S NEWS IS TOO DEPRESSING TO BROADCAST, SO WE'RE RUNNING AN OLD "GILLIGAN'S ISLAND" INSTEAD!
TOM WILSON & TOM II

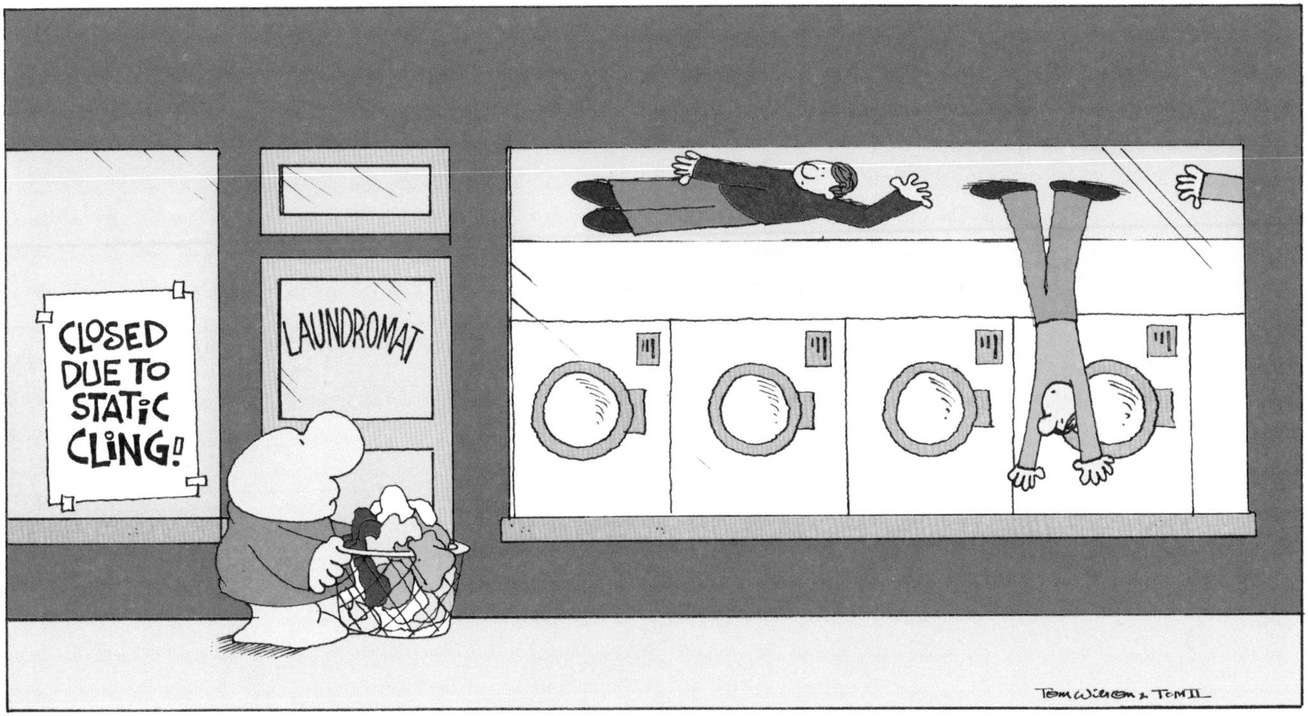
CLOSED DUE TO STATIC CLING!
LAUNDROMAT

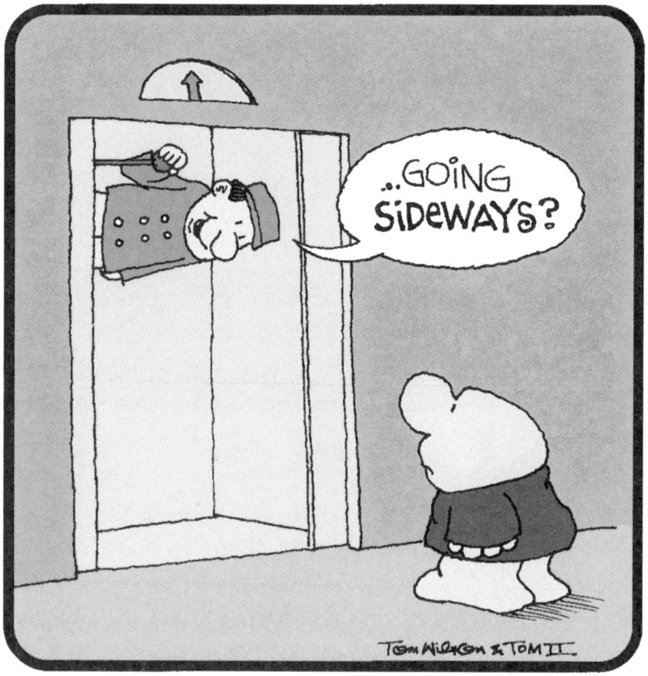
..GOING SIDEWAYS?
TOM WILSON & TOM II

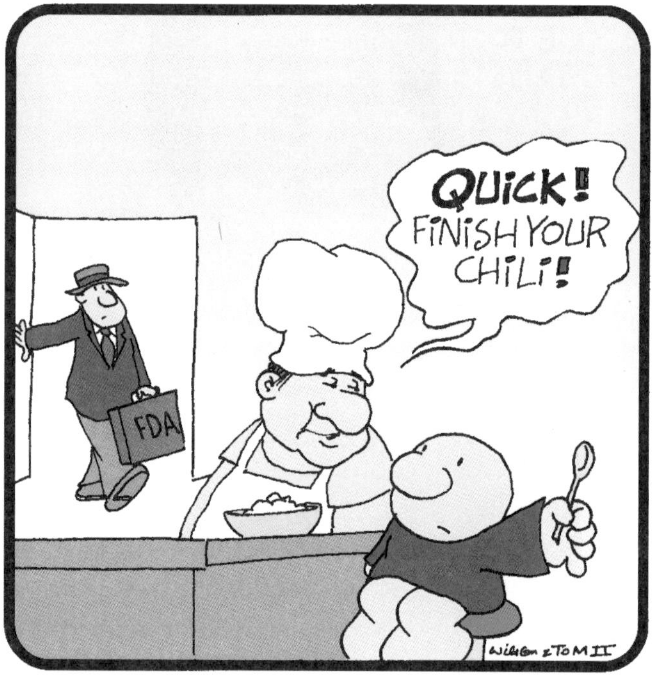
FDA
QUICK! FINISH YOUR CHILI!
WILSON & TOM II

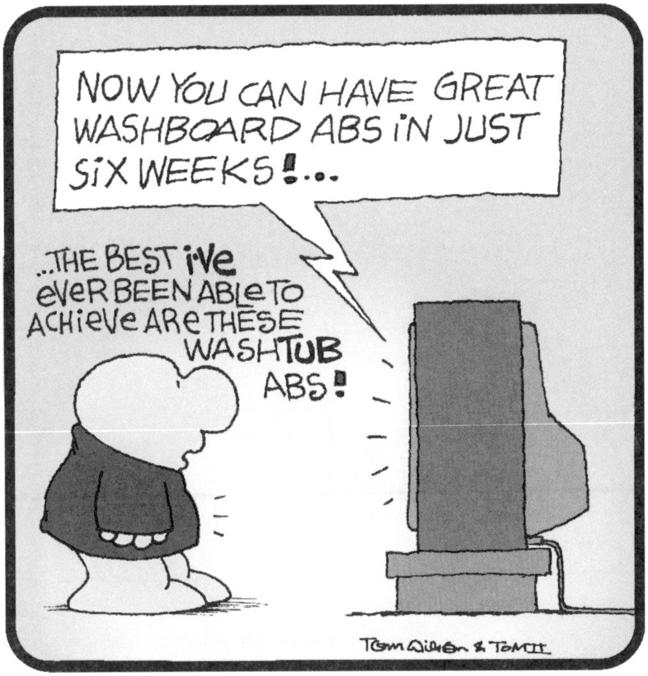
NOW YOU CAN HAVE GREAT WASHBOARD ABS IN JUST SIX WEEKS!...
...THE BEST I'VE EVER BEEN ABLE TO ACHIEVE ARE THESE WASHTUB ABS!
Tom Wilson & Tom II

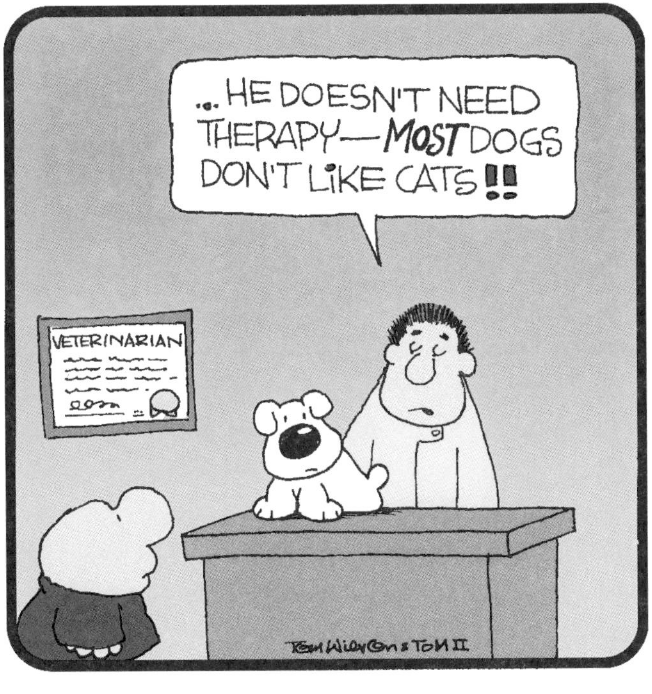
...HE DOESN'T NEED THERAPY—MOST DOGS DON'T LIKE CATS!!
VETERINARIAN
Tom Wilson & Tom II

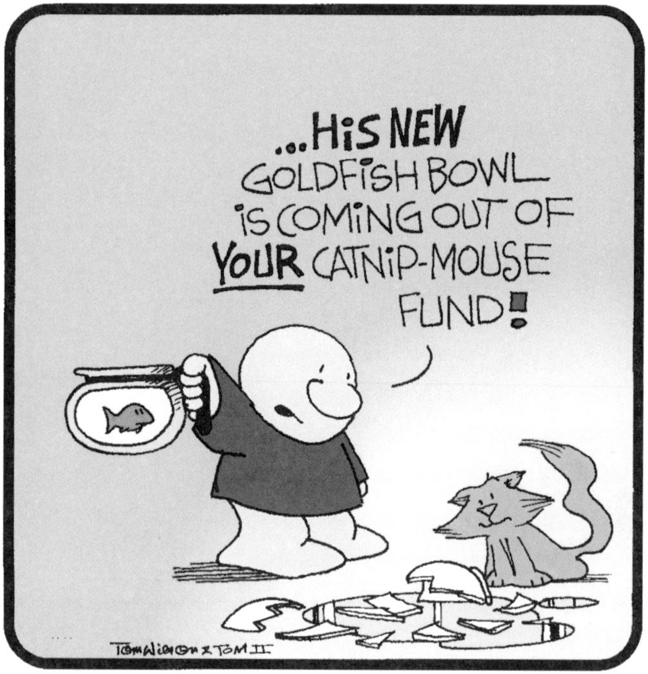
...HiS NEW GOLDFiSH BOWL iS COMiNG OUT OF YOUR CATNiP-MOUSE FUND!

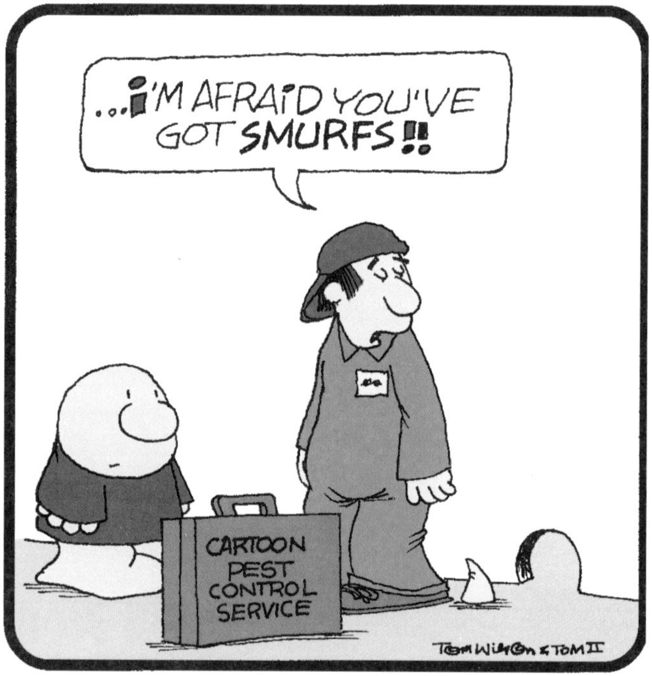
...i'M AFRAiD YOU'VE GOT SMURFS!!
CARTOON PEST CONTROL SERVICE

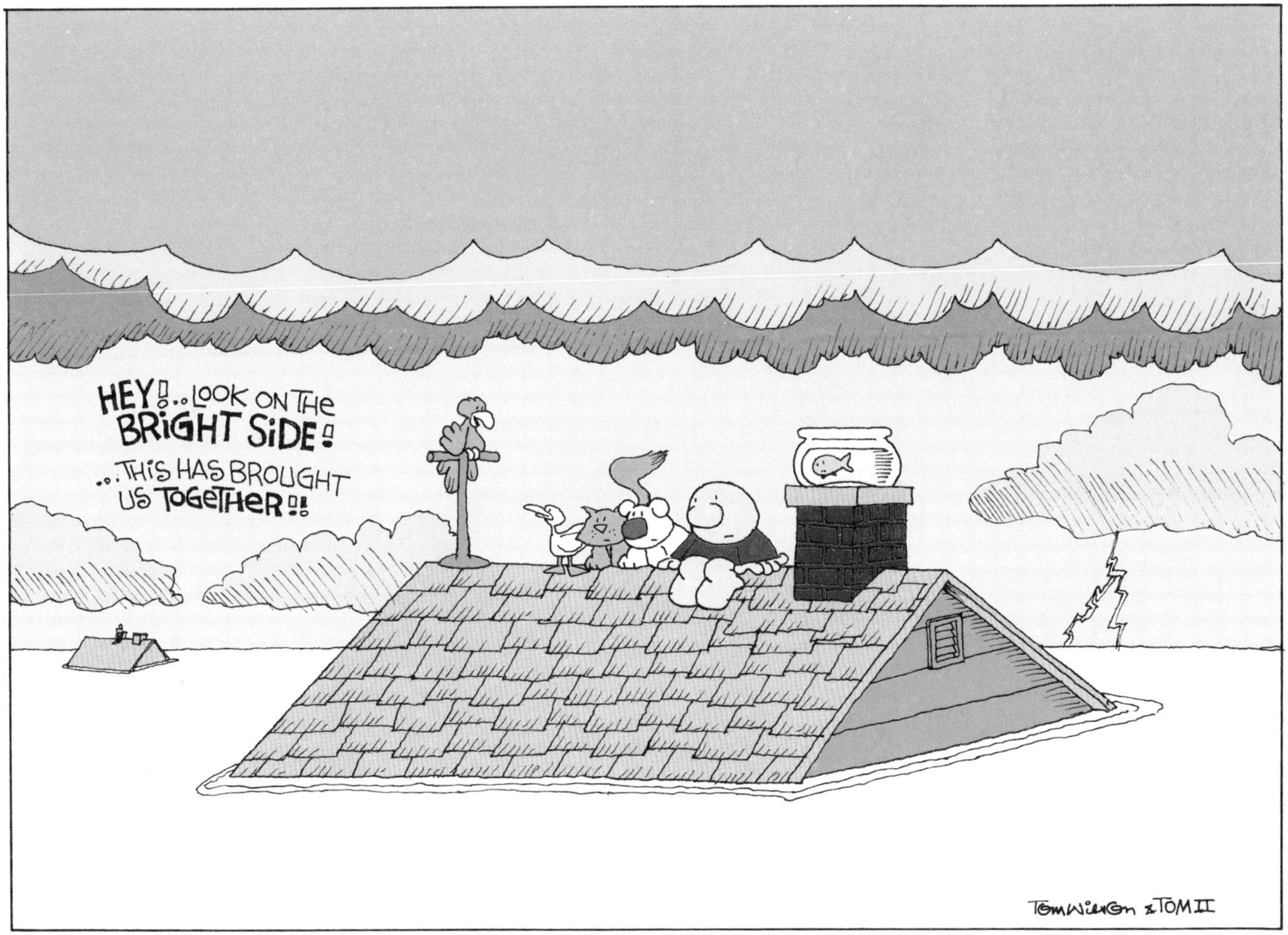
HEY!..LOOK ON THE BRIGHT SIDE!
..THIS HAS BROUGHT US TOGETHER!!
Tom Wilson & TOM II

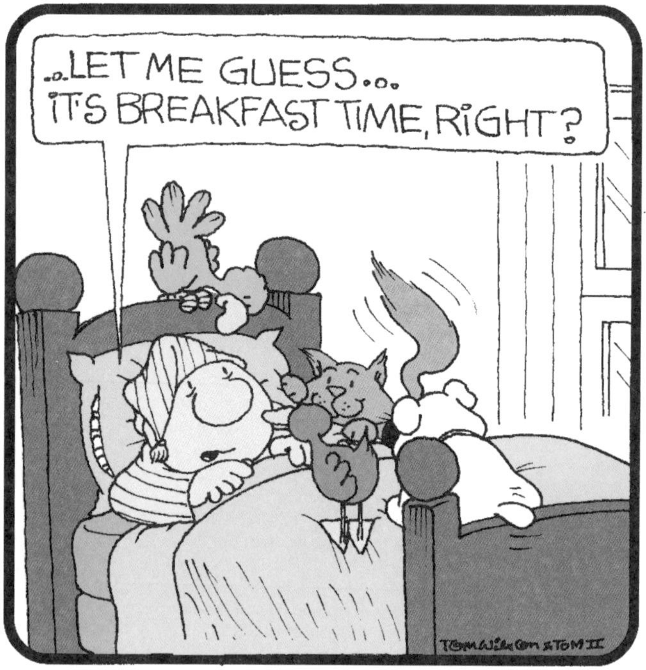
..LET ME GUESS...
IT'S BREAKFAST TIME, RIGHT?
TomWilson & TOM II

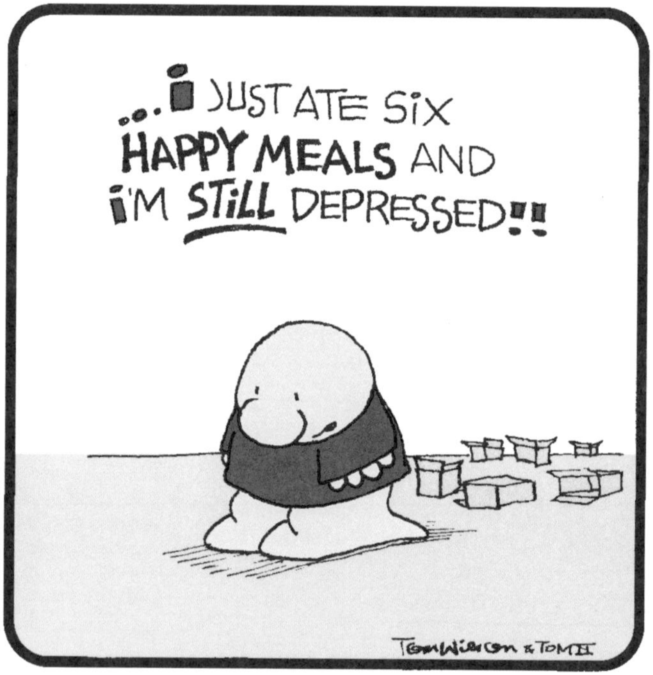
...I JUST ATE SIX HAPPY MEALS AND I'M STILL DEPRESSED!!
TomWilson & TOM II

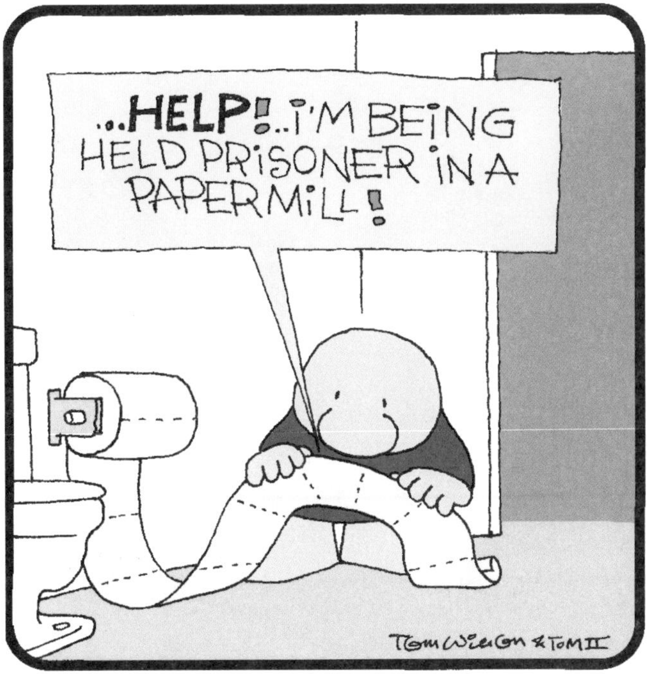
...HELP!..I'M BEING HELD PRISONER IN A PAPER MILL!
TOM WILSON & TOM II

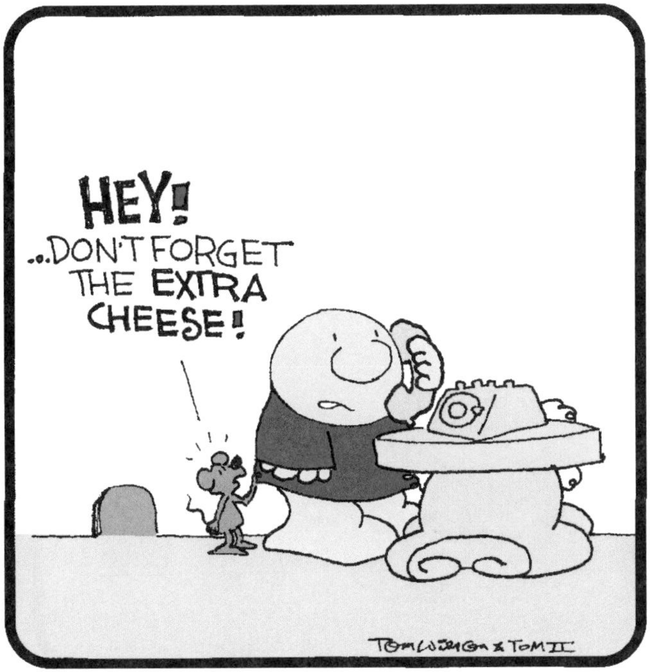
HEY! ...DON'T FORGET THE EXTRA CHEESE!
TOM WILSON & TOM II

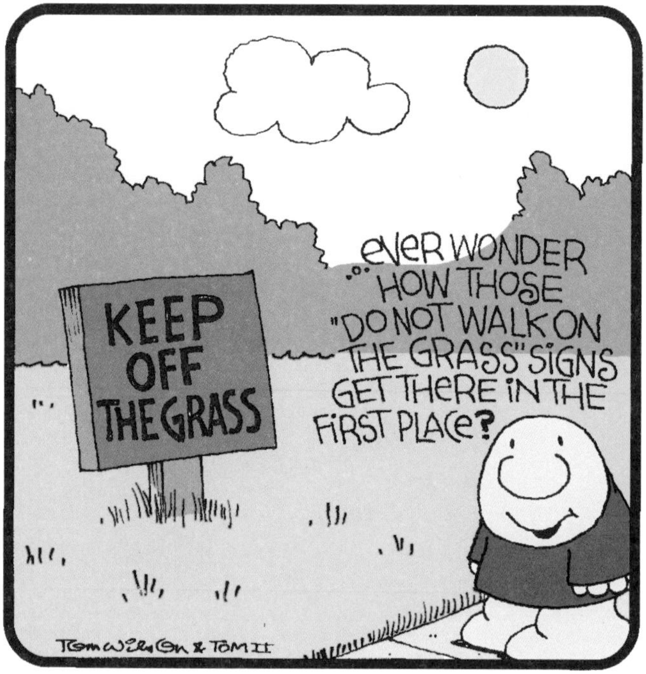
KEEP OFF THE GRASS
...EVER WONDER HOW THOSE "DO NOT WALK ON THE GRASS" SIGNS GET THERE IN THE FIRST PLACE?
TOM WILSON & TOM II

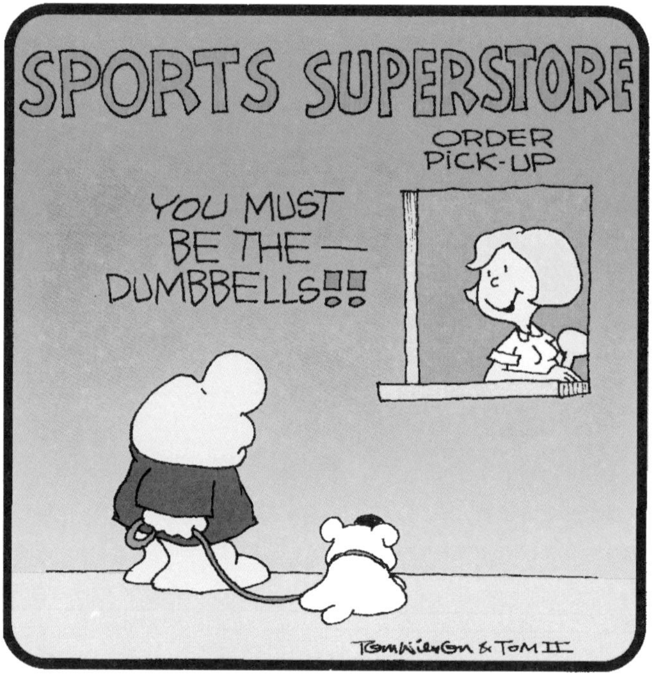
SPORTS SUPERSTORE
ORDER PICK-UP
YOU MUST BE THE — DUMBBELLS!!
TOM WILSON & TOM II

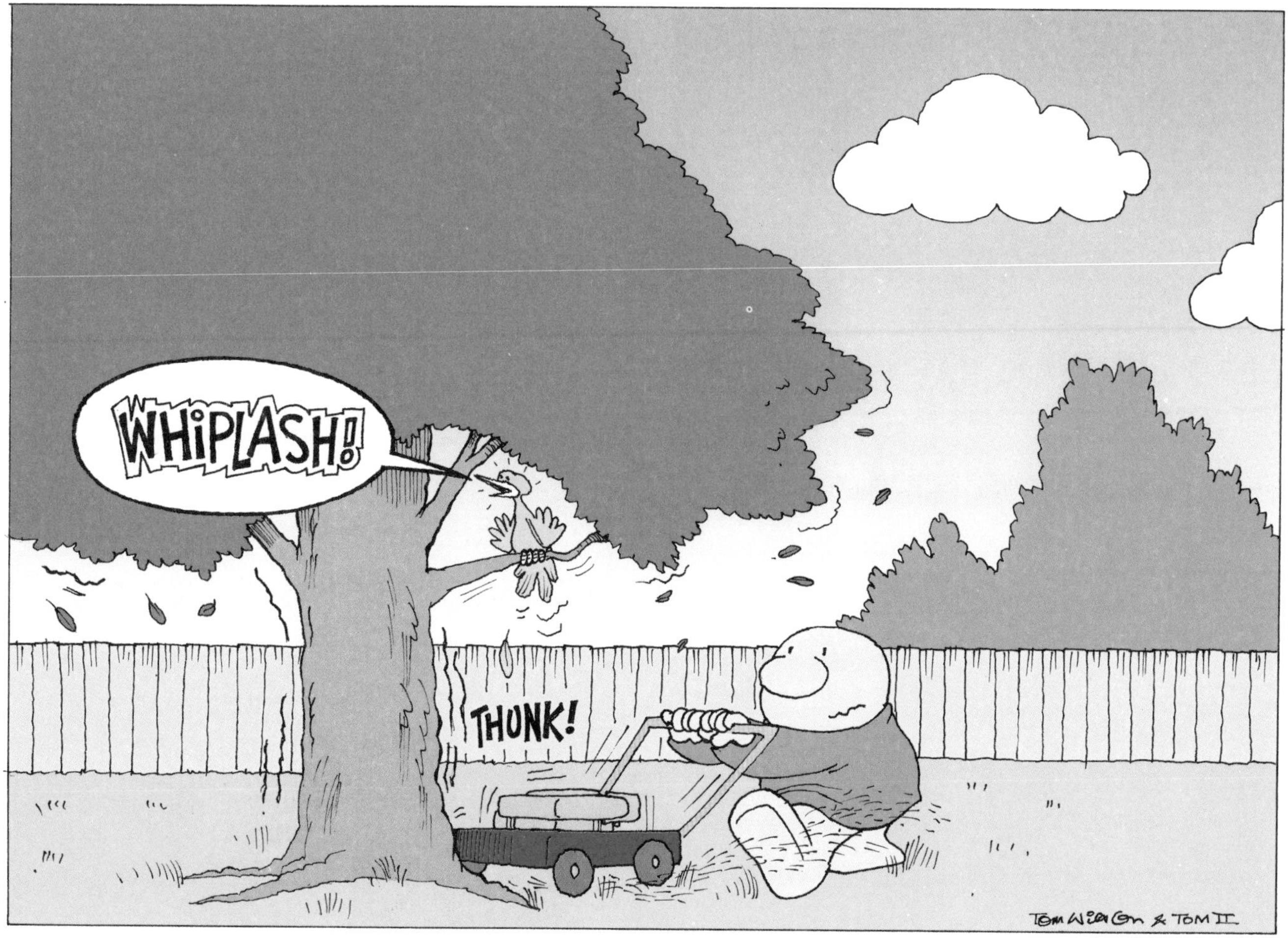
WHIPLASH!
THUNK!
TOM WILSON & TOM II

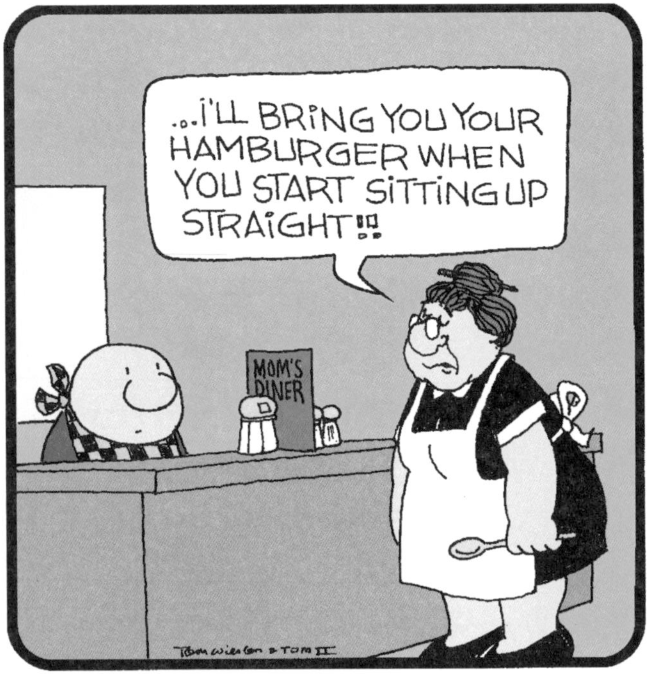
...I'LL BRING YOU YOUR HAMBURGER WHEN YOU START SITTING UP STRAIGHT!!
MOM'S DINER

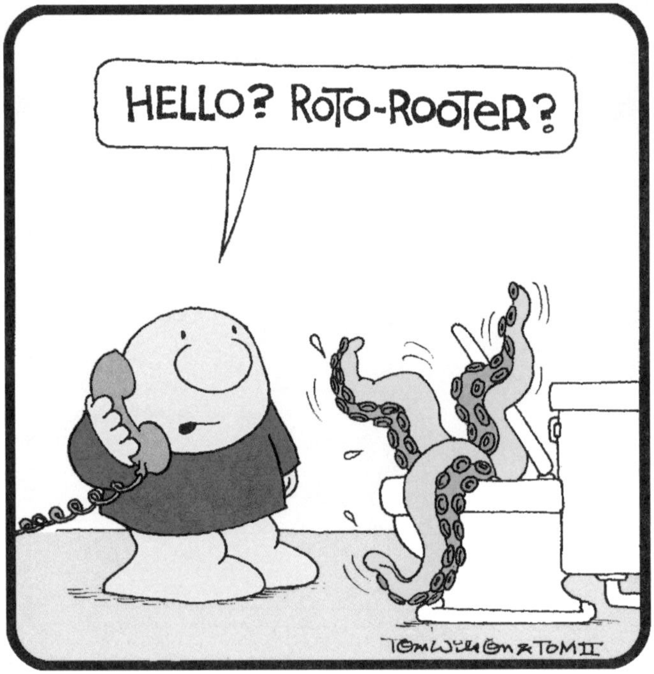
HELLO? ROTO-ROOTER?

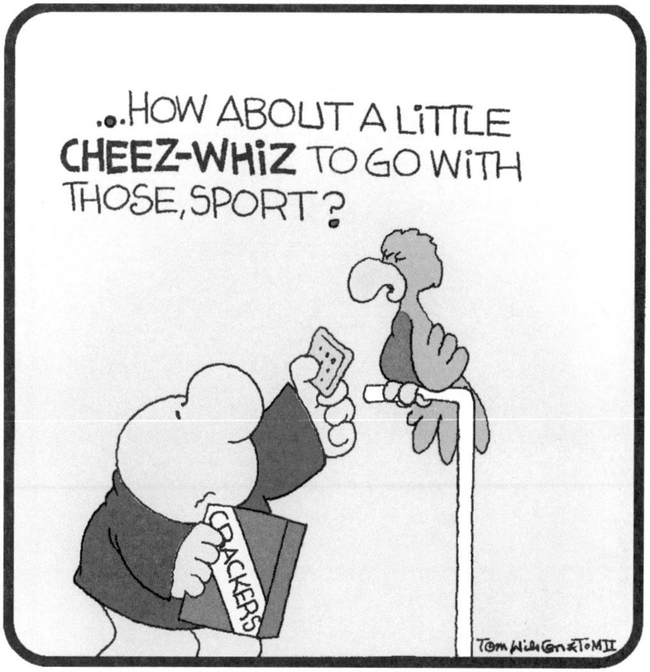
..HOW ABOUT A LITTLE CHEEZ-WHIZ TO GO WITH THOSE, SPORT?
CRACKERS
TOM WILSON & TOM II

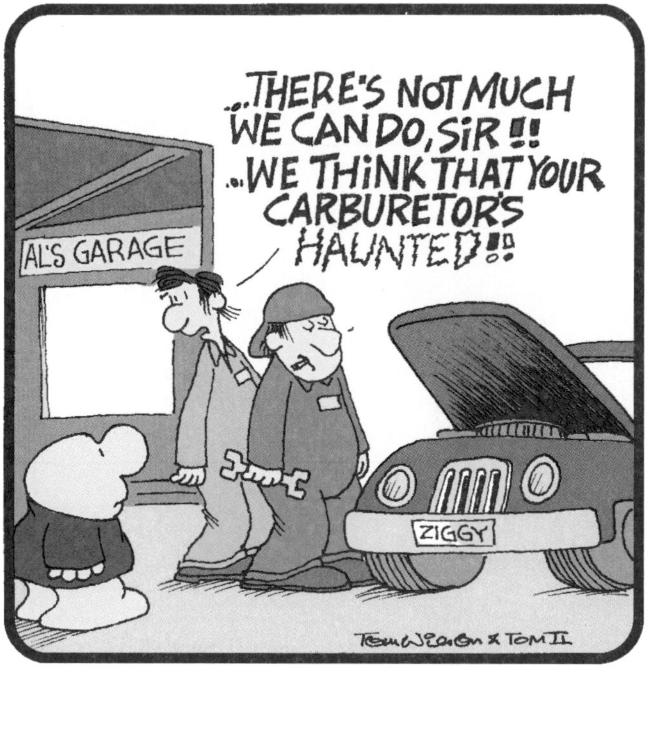
..THERE'S NOT MUCH WE CAN DO, SIR!! ..WE THINK THAT YOUR CARBURETOR'S HAUNTED!!
AL'S GARAGE
ZIGGY
TOM WILSON & TOM II

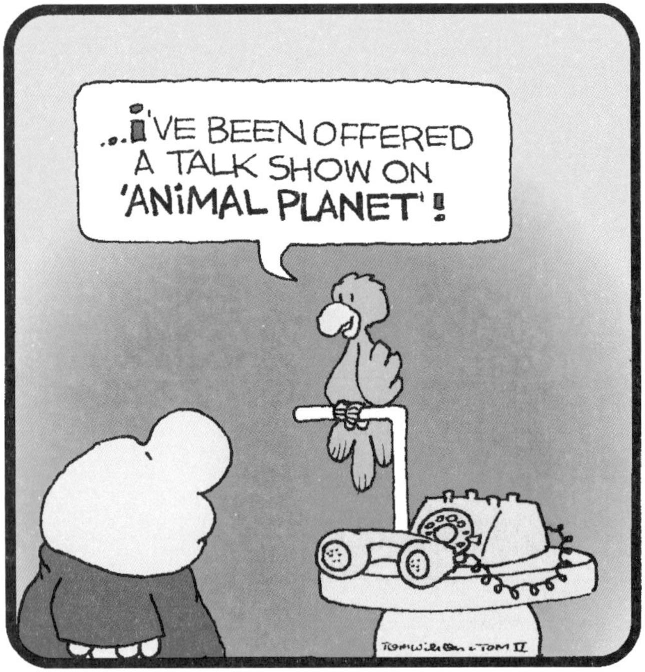
..I'VE BEEN OFFERED A TALK SHOW ON 'ANIMAL PLANET'!
TOM WILSON & TOM II

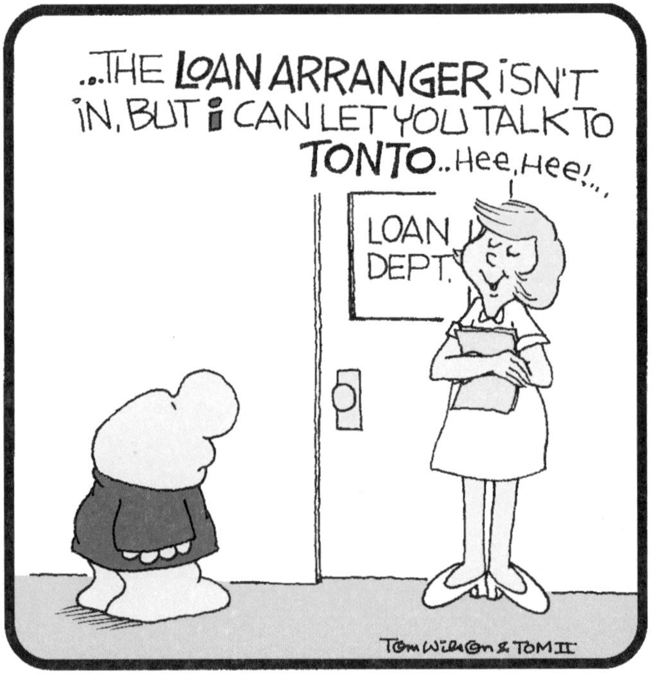
..THE LOAN ARRANGER ISN'T IN, BUT I CAN LET YOU TALK TO TONTO..Hee, Hee!..
LOAN DEPT.
TOM WILSON & TOM II

?
?
Nope
NOT HERE!
ZIGGY
NOT HERE!!
..o.. THERE YOU ARE!! I'VE BEEN LOOKING EVERYWHERE FOR YOU!!
LOVE
Tom Wilson & Tom II

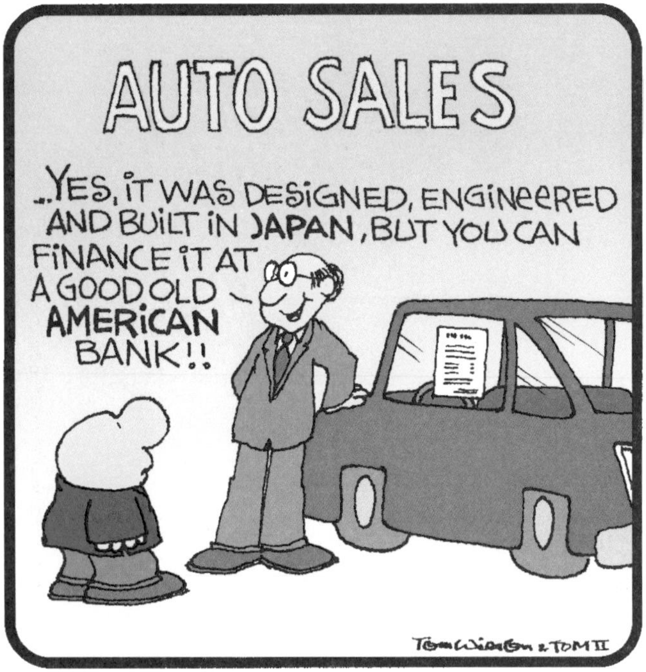
AUTO SALES
...YES, IT WAS DESIGNED, ENGINEERED AND BUILT IN JAPAN, BUT YOU CAN FINANCE IT AT A GOOD OLD AMERICAN BANK!!
TOM WILSON & TOM II

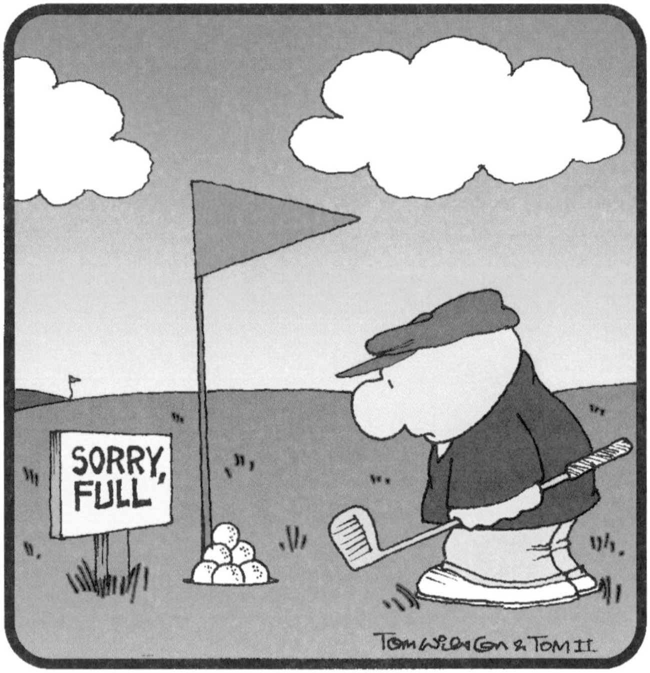
SORRY, FULL
TOM WILSON & TOM II

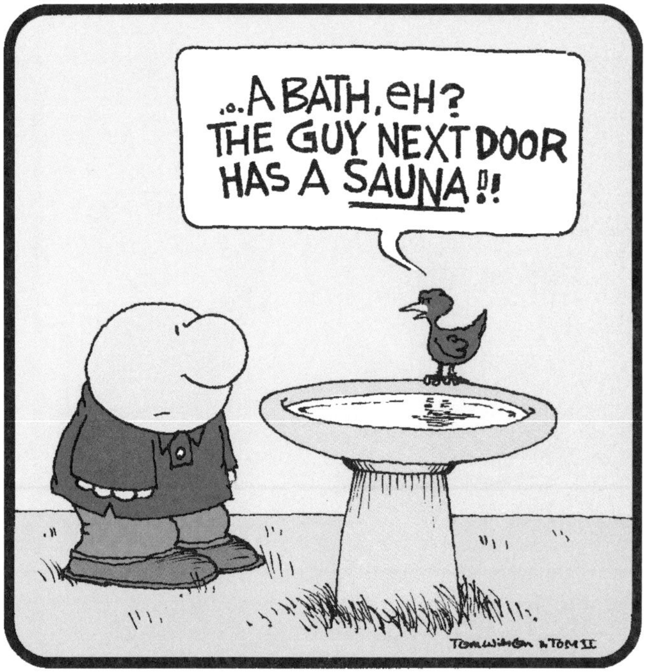
..A BATH, eH? THE GUY NEXT DOOR HAS A SAUNA!!
TOM WILSON & TOM II

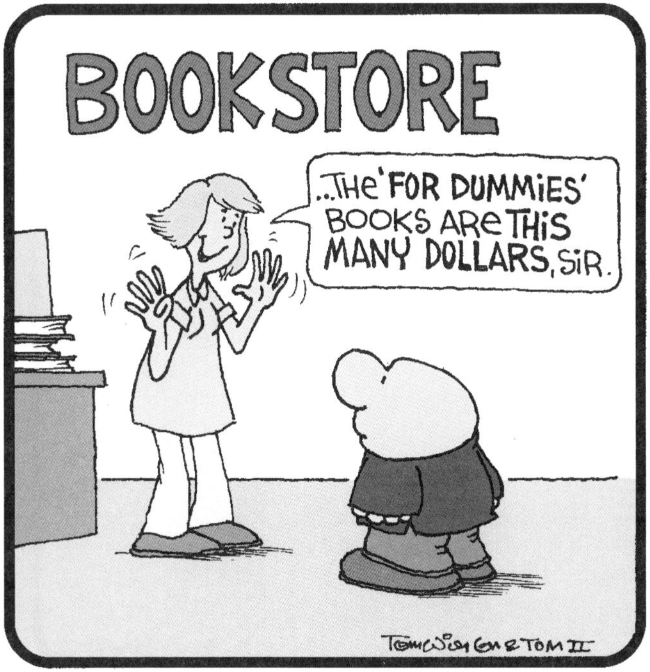
BOOKSTORE
..THE 'FOR DUMMIES' BOOKS ARE THIS MANY DOLLARS, SIR.
TOM WILSON & TOM II

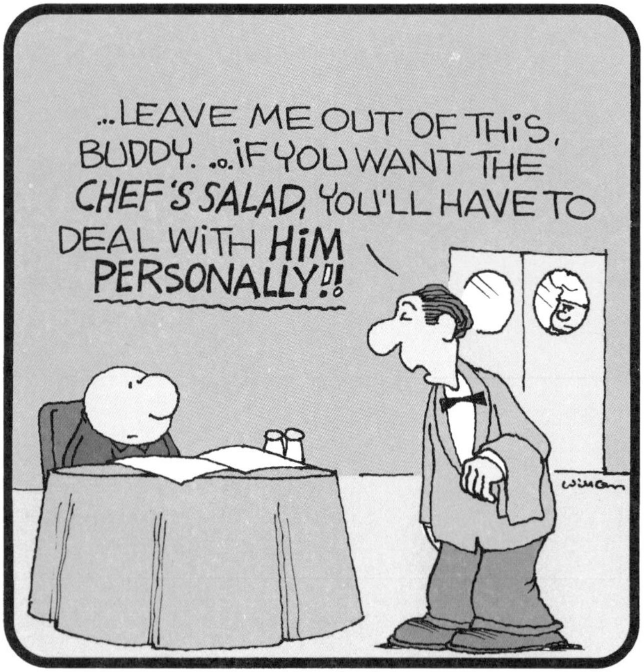
...LEAVE ME OUT OF THIS, BUDDY. ..o. IF YOU WANT THE CHEF'S SALAD, YOU'LL HAVE TO DEAL WITH HIM PERSONALLY?!!

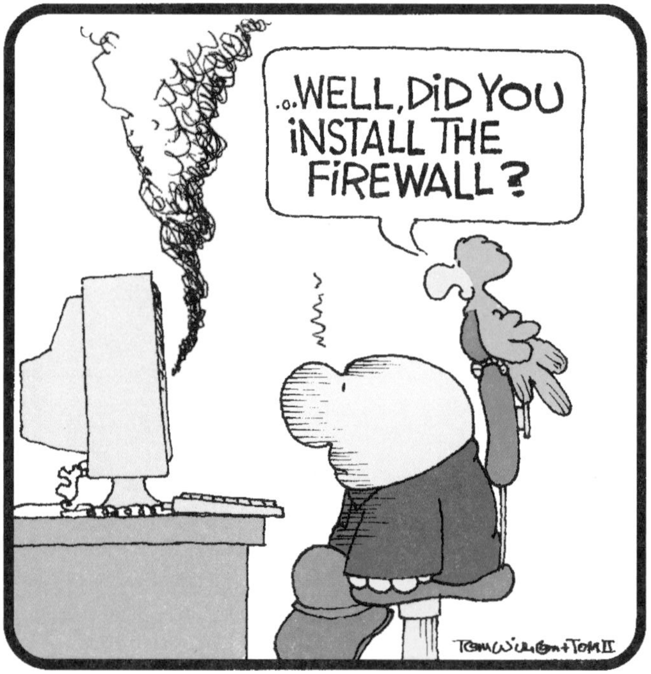
.o. WELL, DID YOU INSTALL THE FIREWALL?

...SOMETIMES WE IMAGINE THAT THE WORLD IS SO BIG...

..AND SOMETIMES WHEN THAT HAPPENS IT MAKES US FEEL SO SMALL...

..THAT'S WHEN WE GET AFRAID AND FEEL SO HELPLESS...

..AND SOMETIMES WE FORGET...

..THAT THE WORLD IS ONLY AS BIG AS WE IMAGINE IT IS... AND WE ARE ONLY AS SMALL AS WE IMAGINE WE ARE...

..SO REMEMBER THAT WHEN THE WORLD MAKES US FEEL AFRAID AND HELPLESS... ITS JUST OUR IMAGINATION!!

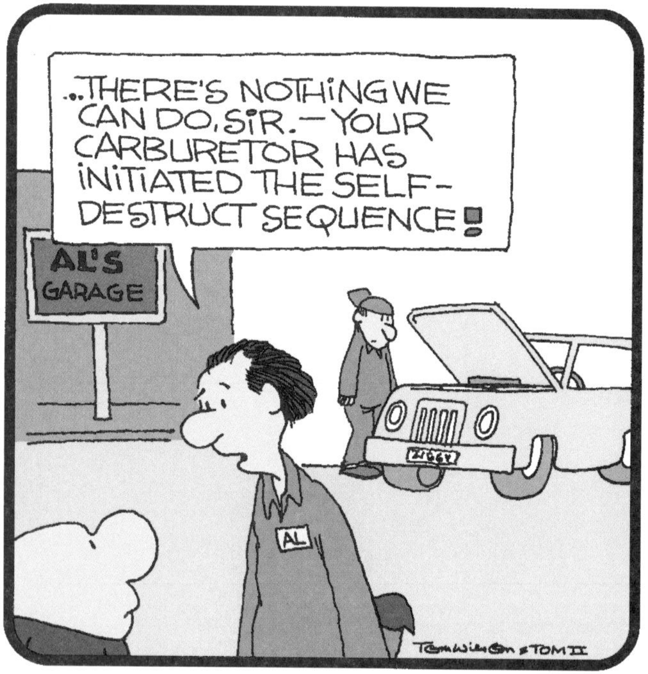
..THERE'S NOTHING WE CAN DO, SIR.—YOUR CARBURETOR HAS INITIATED THE SELF-DESTRUCT SEQUENCE!
AL'S GARAGE
AL
ZIGGY

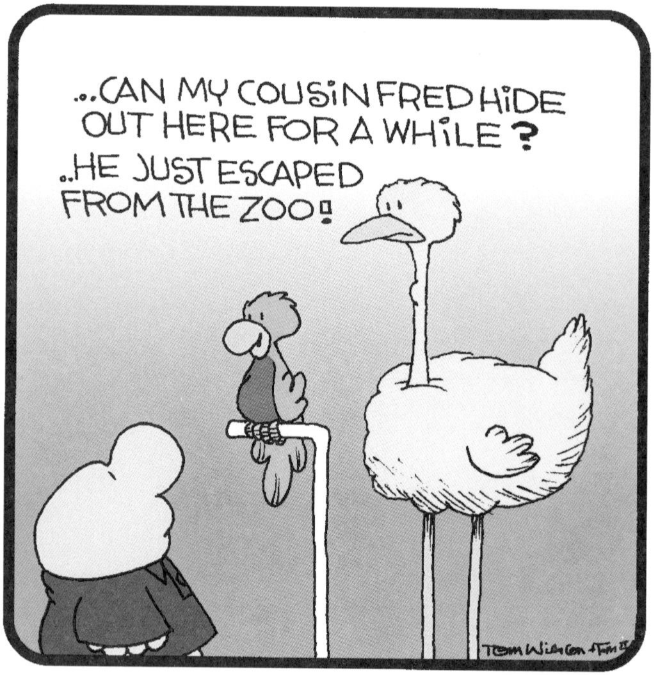
...CAN MY COUSIN FRED HIDE OUT HERE FOR A WHILE? ..HE JUST ESCAPED FROM THE ZOO!

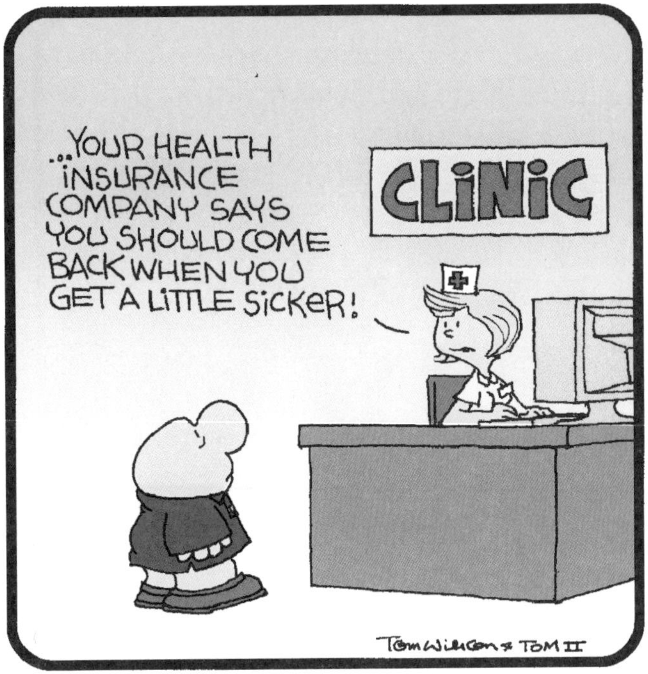
...YOUR HEALTH INSURANCE COMPANY SAYS YOU SHOULD COME BACK WHEN YOU GET A LITTLE SICKER!
CLINIC
Tom Wilson & Tom II

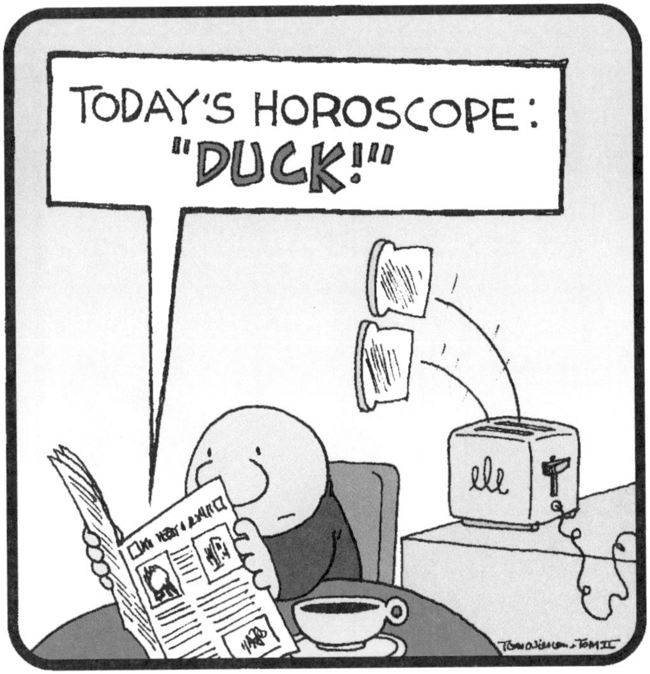
TODAY'S HOROSCOPE: "DUCK!"
Tom Wilson & Tom II

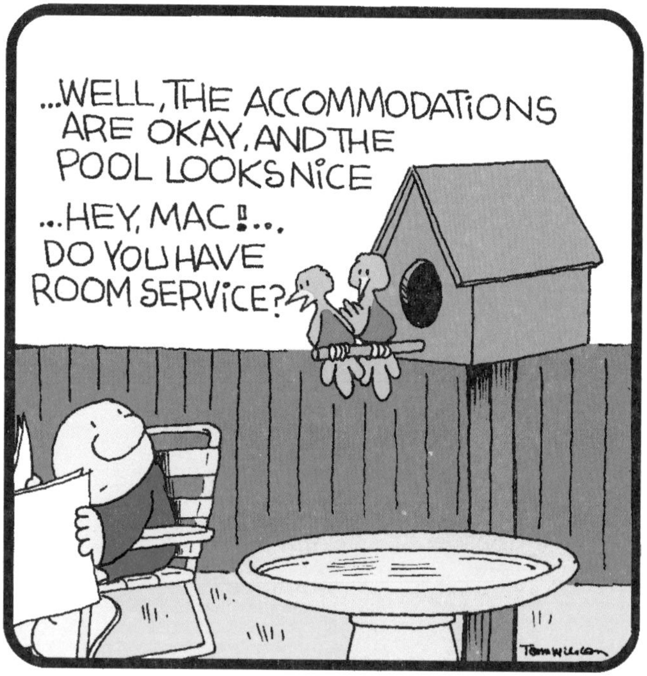
...WELL, THE ACCOMMODATIONS ARE OKAY, AND THE POOL LOOKS NICE
...HEY, MAC!... DO YOU HAVE ROOM SERVICE?

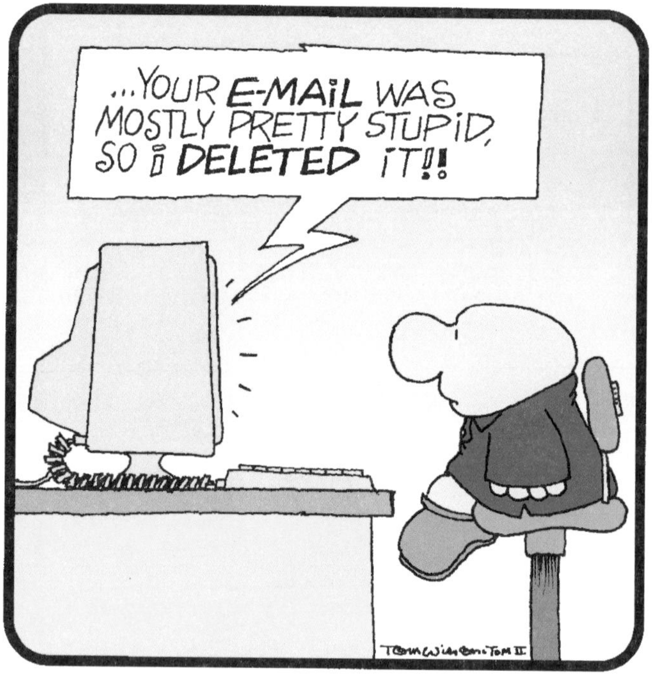
...YOUR E-MAIL WAS MOSTLY PRETTY STUPID, SO I DELETED IT!!

..OKAY! HEAD DOWN...KNEES BENT...RELAX...
SWING
HHMMM!
...WELL, I THINK I SEE YOUR PROBLEM...
REALLY?
YEAH..YOU'RE STANDING TOO CLOSE TO THE BALL!!
...AFTER YOU HIT IT!!
TOM WILSON & TOM II

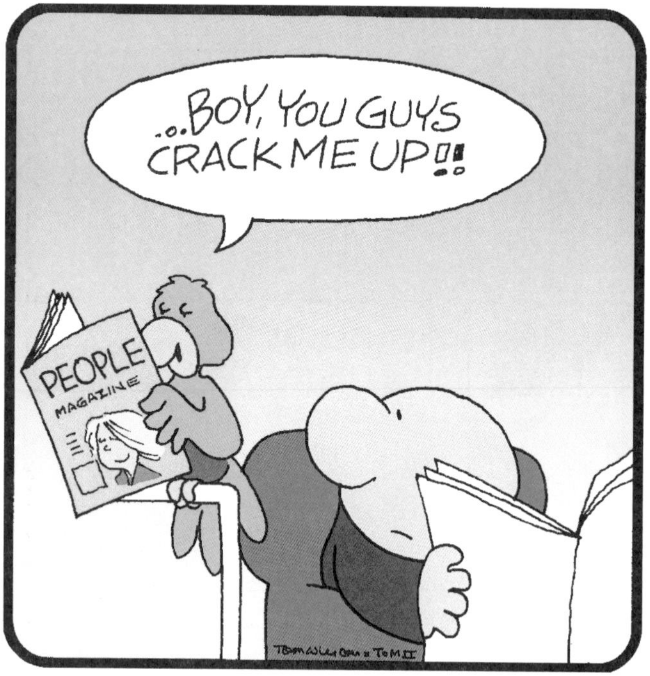
..BOY, YOU GUYS CRACK ME UP!!
PEOPLE MAGAZINE

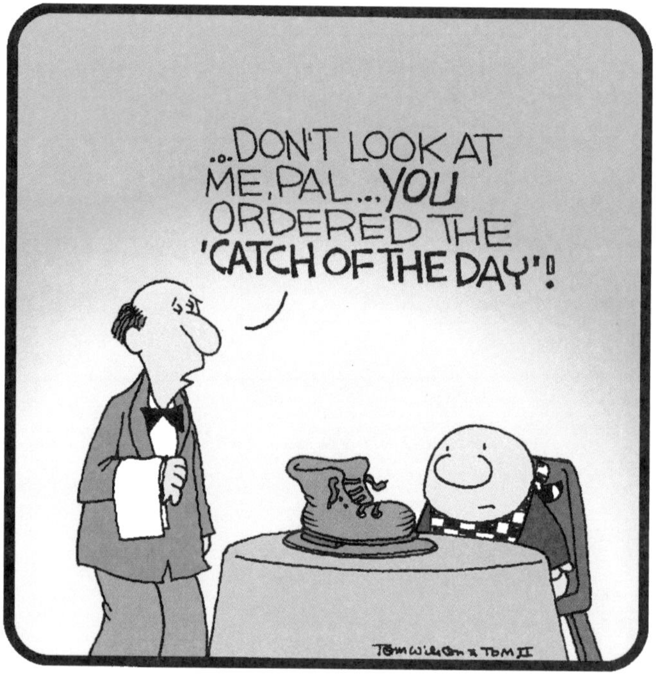
..DON'T LOOK AT ME, PAL...YOU ORDERED THE "CATCH OF THE DAY"!

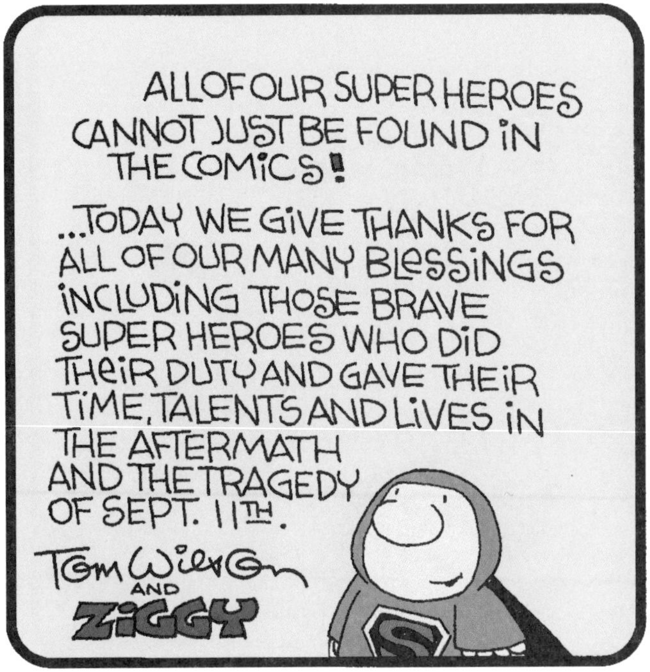
ALL OF OUR SUPER HEROES CANNOT JUST BE FOUND IN THE COMICS!
...TODAY WE GIVE THANKS FOR ALL OF OUR MANY BLESSINGS INCLUDING THOSE BRAVE SUPER HEROES WHO DID THEIR DUTY AND GAVE THEIR TIME, TALENTS AND LIVES IN THE AFTERMATH AND THE TRAGEDY OF SEPT. 11TH.
TOM WILSON AND ZIGGY

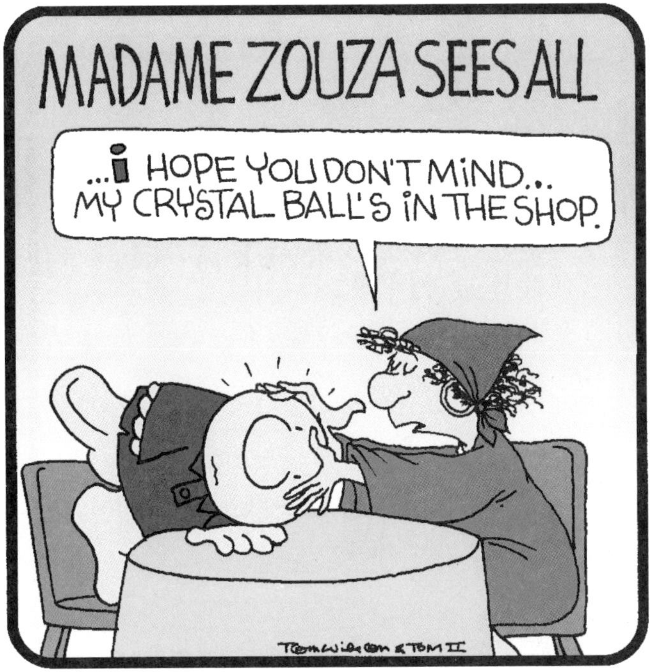
MADAME ZOUZA SEES ALL
...I HOPE YOU DON'T MIND... MY CRYSTAL BALL'S IN THE SHOP.
TOM WILSON & TOM II

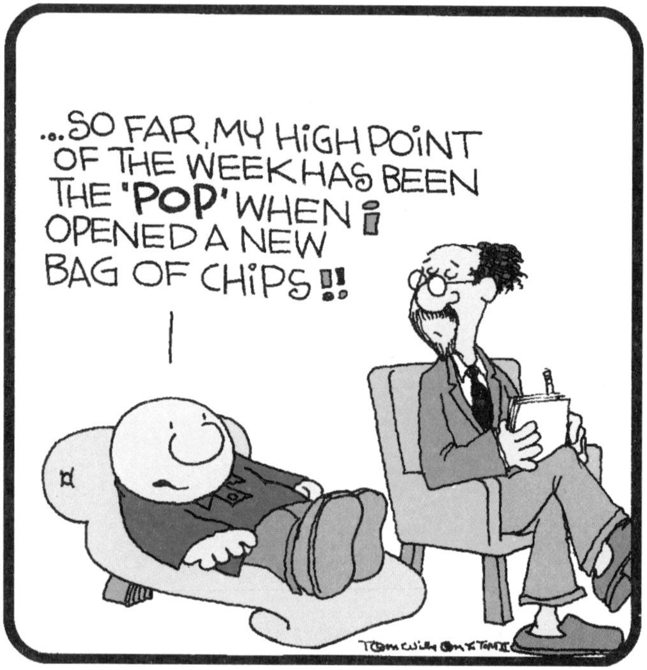
...SO FAR, MY HIGH POINT OF THE WEEK HAS BEEN THE 'POP' WHEN I OPENED A NEW BAG OF CHIPS!!

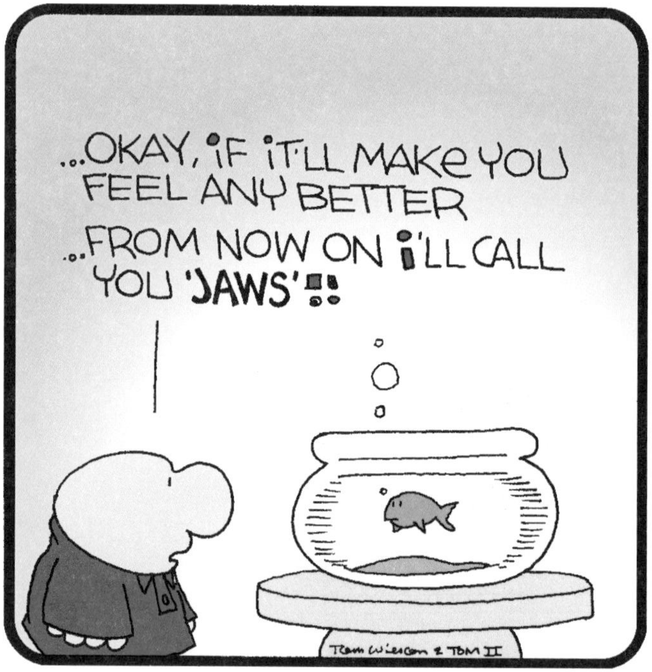
...OKAY, IF IT'LL MAKE YOU FEEL ANY BETTER
...FROM NOW ON I'LL CALL YOU 'JAWS'!!

LOVERS LANE
LOVE AND KISSES
...BEING ALONE WOULDN'T BE SUCH A LONELY THING...
...IF ONLY I COULD FIND SOMEONE TO SHARE IT WITH!!
...FOR SARAH

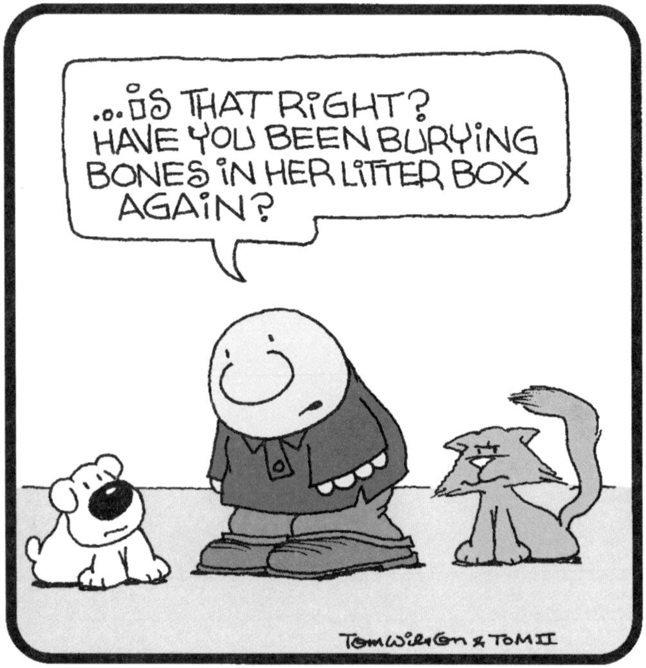
...IS THAT RIGHT? HAVE YOU BEEN BURYING BONES IN HER LITTER BOX AGAIN?
TOM WILSON & TOM II

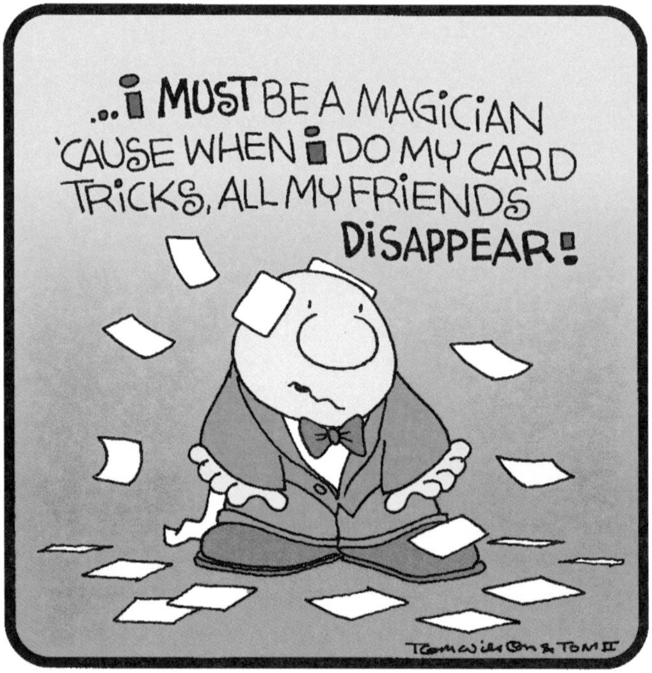
...I MUST BE A MAGICIAN 'CAUSE WHEN I DO MY CARD TRICKS, ALL MY FRIENDS DISAPPEAR!
TOM WILSON & TOM II

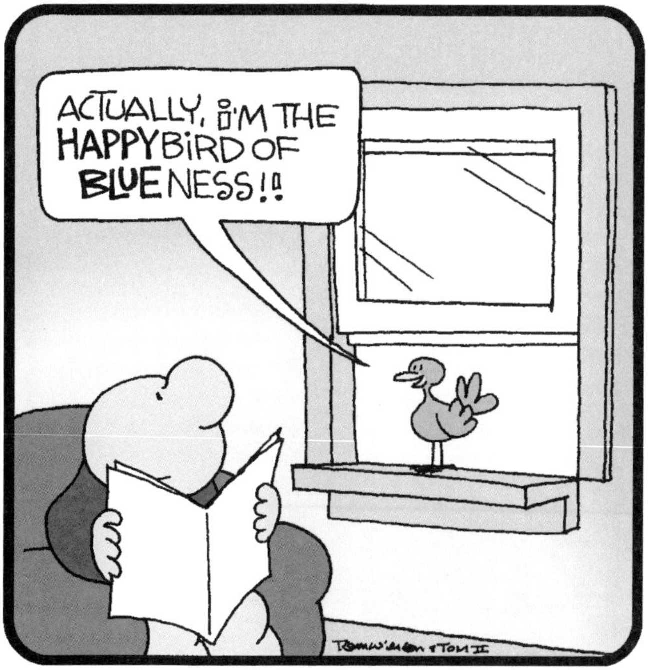
ACTUALLY, I'M THE HAPPY BIRD OF BLUENESS!!

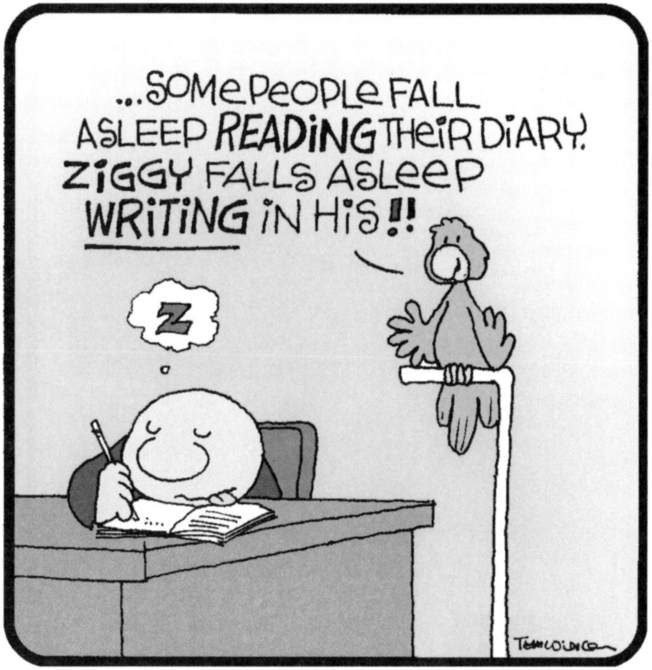
...SOME PEOPLE FALL ASLEEP READING THEIR DIARY. ZIGGY FALLS ASLEEP WRITING IN HIS!!
Z

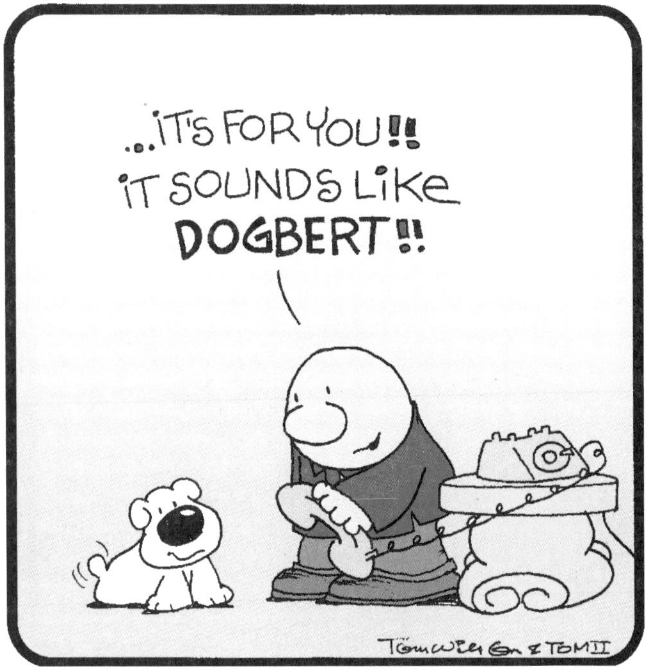
...IT'S FOR YOU!!
IT SOUNDS LIKE
DOGBERT!!
TOM WILSON & TOM II

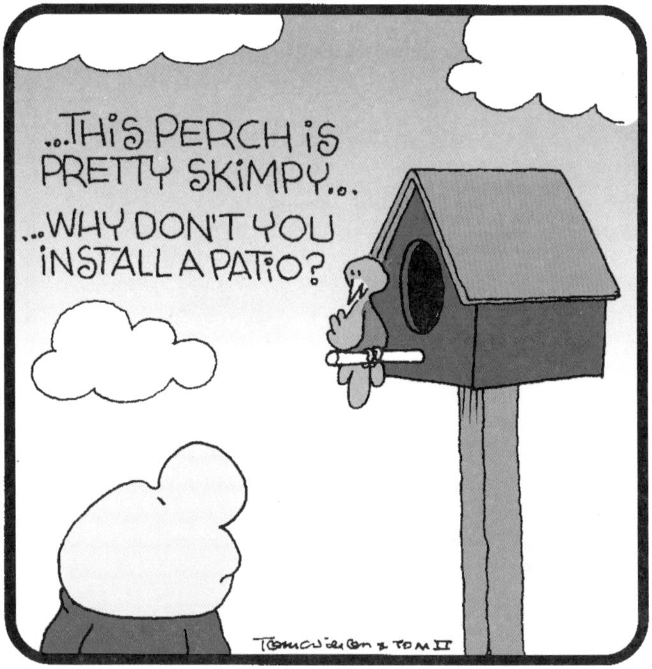
...THIS PERCH IS PRETTY SKIMPY...
...WHY DON'T YOU INSTALL A PATIO?
TOM WILSON & TOM II

..KIDS HAVE SO MANY CHOICES THESE DAYS!
SOME MAY BECOME POLICEMEN OR FIREMEN...
...SOME WANT TO GROW UP TO BE DOCTORS OR CONSTRUCTION WORKERS.
...AND SOME MIGHT EVEN BECOME CARTOONISTS!!
ME?
...I ALWAYS WANTED TO BE A KID WHEN I GREW UP!

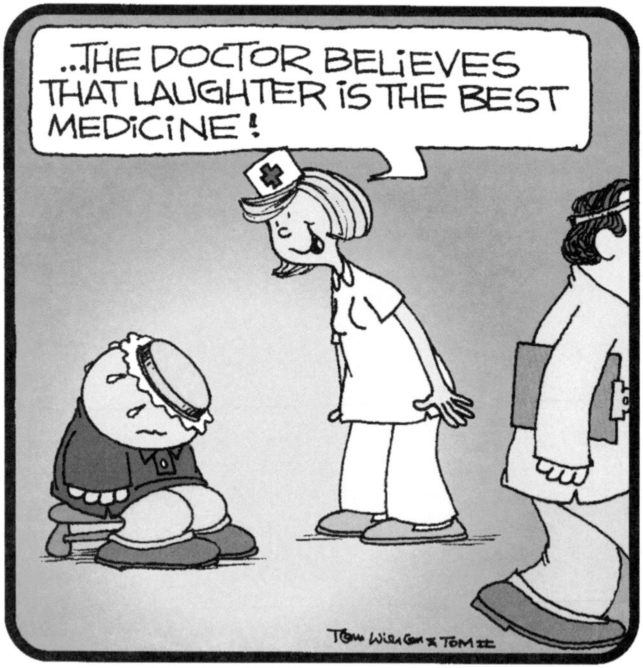
..THE DOCTOR BELIEVES THAT LAUGHTER IS THE BEST MEDICINE!
TOM WILSON & TOM II

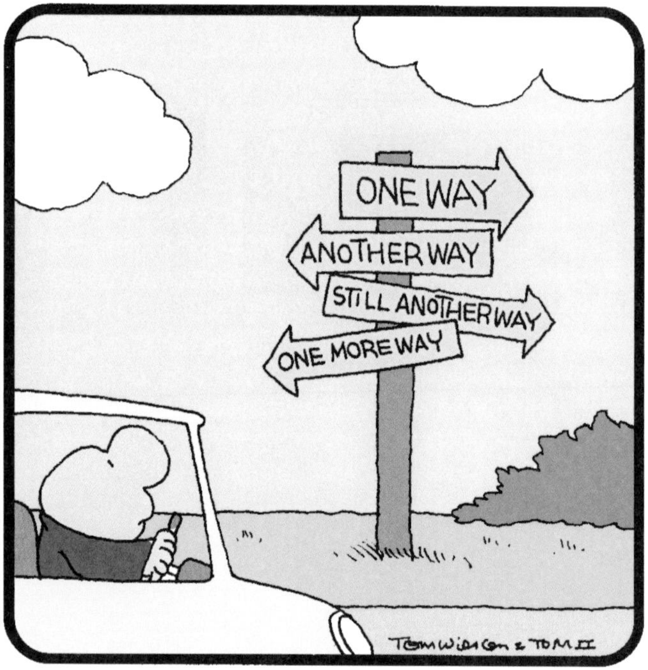
ONE WAY
ANOTHER WAY
STILL ANOTHER WAY
ONE MORE WAY
TOM WILSON & TOM II

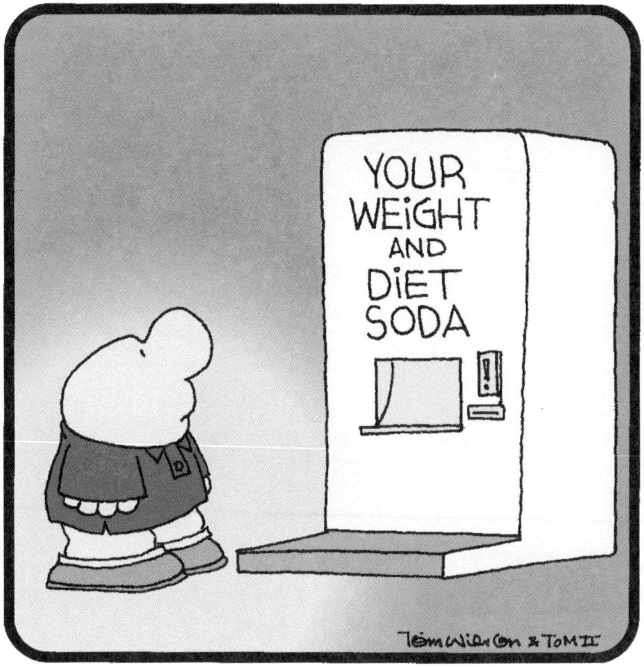
YOUR WEIGHT AND DIET SODA
Tom Wilson & TOM II

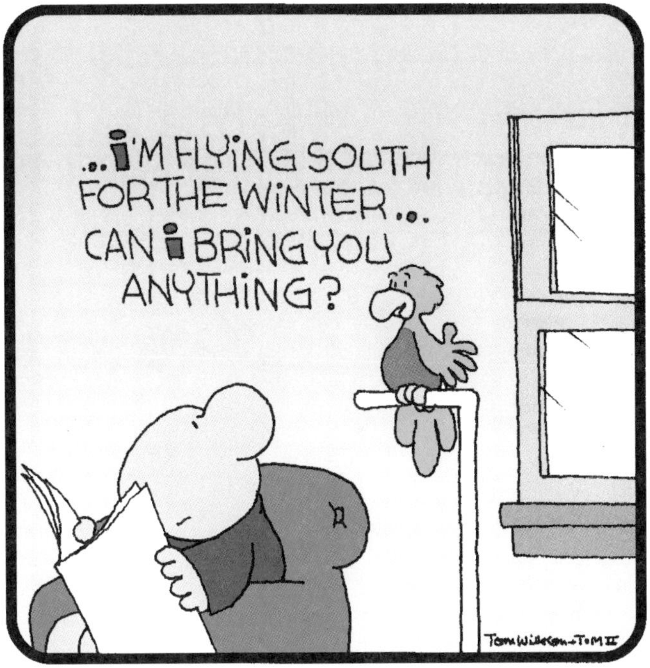
...I'M FLYING SOUTH FOR THE WINTER... CAN I BRING YOU ANYTHING?
Tom Wilson & TOM II

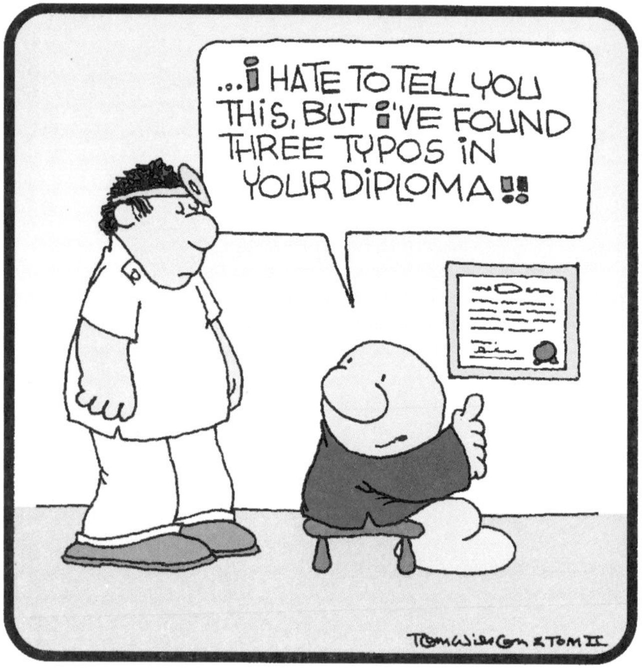
...I HATE TO TELL YOU THIS, BUT I'VE FOUND THREE TYPOS IN YOUR DIPLOMA!!
TOM WILSON & TOM II

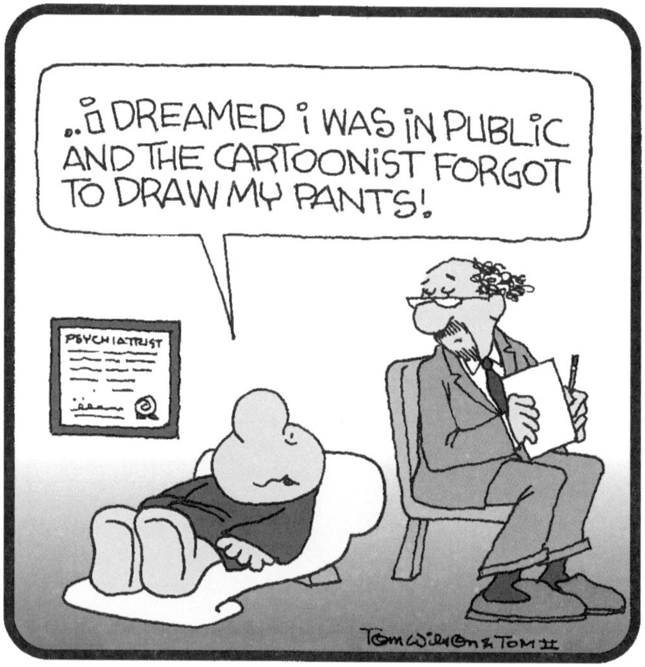
..I DREAMED I WAS IN PUBLIC AND THE CARTOONIST FORGOT TO DRAW MY PANTS!
PSYCHIATRIST
TOM WILSON & TOM II

BLUB
!!!
STAFF
?
BLUB
TOM WILSON & TOM II

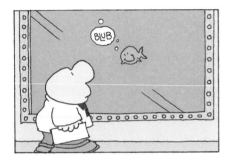

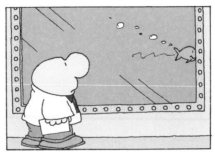

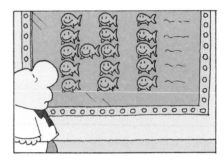

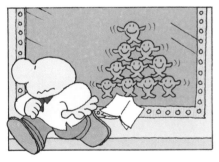

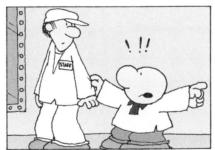

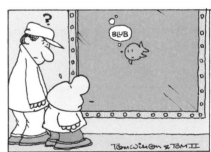

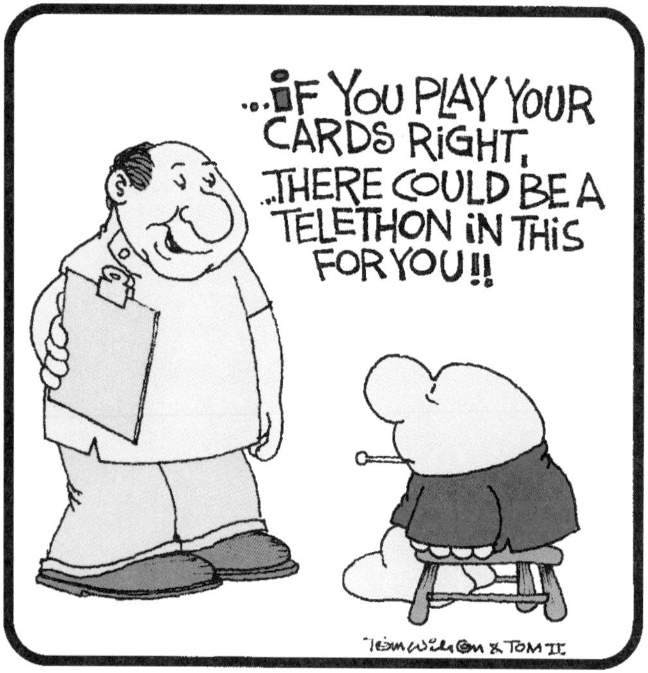
...IF YOU PLAY YOUR CARDS RIGHT, ...THERE COULD BE A TELETHON IN THIS FOR YOU!!
TOM WILSON & TOM II

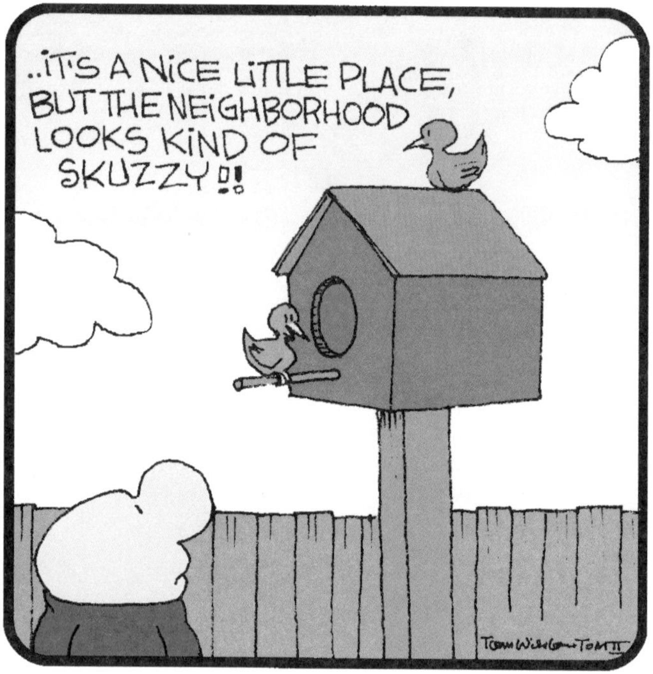
...IT'S A NICE LITTLE PLACE, BUT THE NEIGHBORHOOD LOOKS KIND OF SKUZZY!!
TOM WILSON TOM II

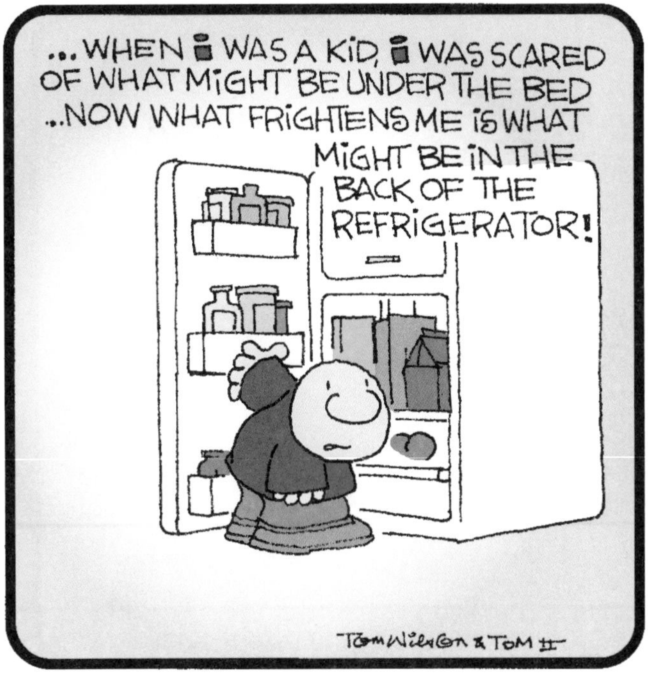
...WHEN I WAS A KID, I WAS SCARED OF WHAT MIGHT BE UNDER THE BED ...NOW WHAT FRIGHTENS ME IS WHAT MIGHT BE IN THE BACK OF THE REFRIGERATOR!
Tom Wilson & Tom II

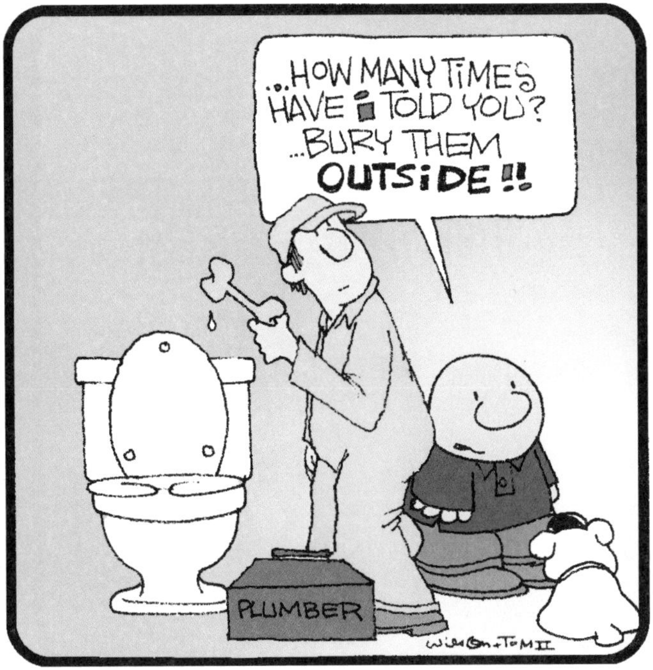
...HOW MANY TIMES HAVE I TOLD YOU? ...BURY THEM OUTSIDE!!
PLUMBER
Wilson+Tom II

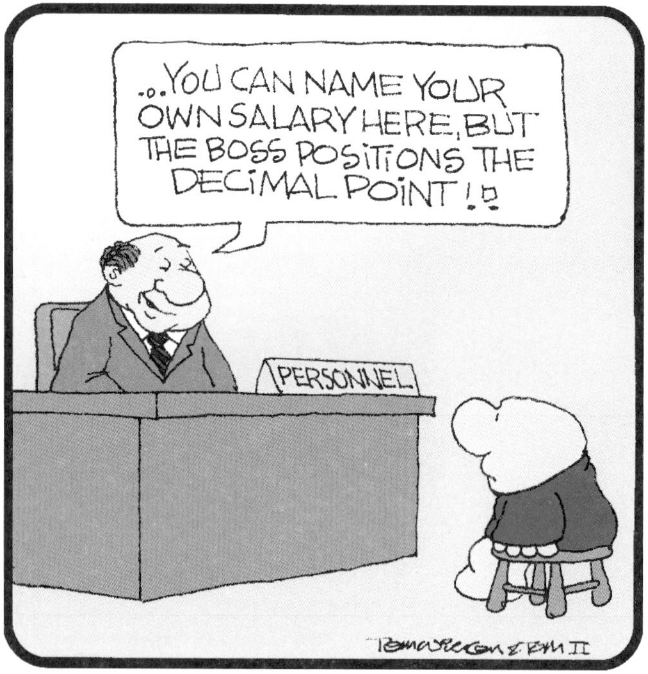
...YOU CAN NAME YOUR OWN SALARY HERE, BUT THE BOSS POSITIONS THE DECIMAL POINT!!
PERSONNEL

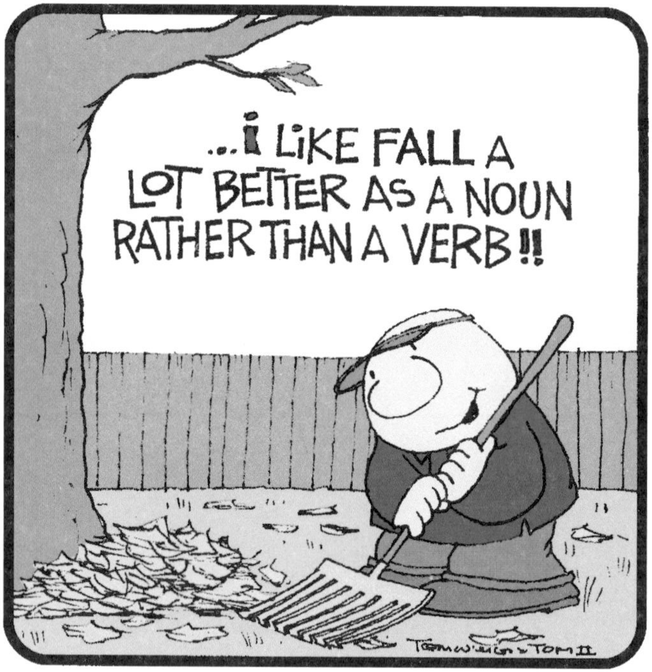
...I LIKE FALL A LOT BETTER AS A NOUN RATHER THAN A VERB!!

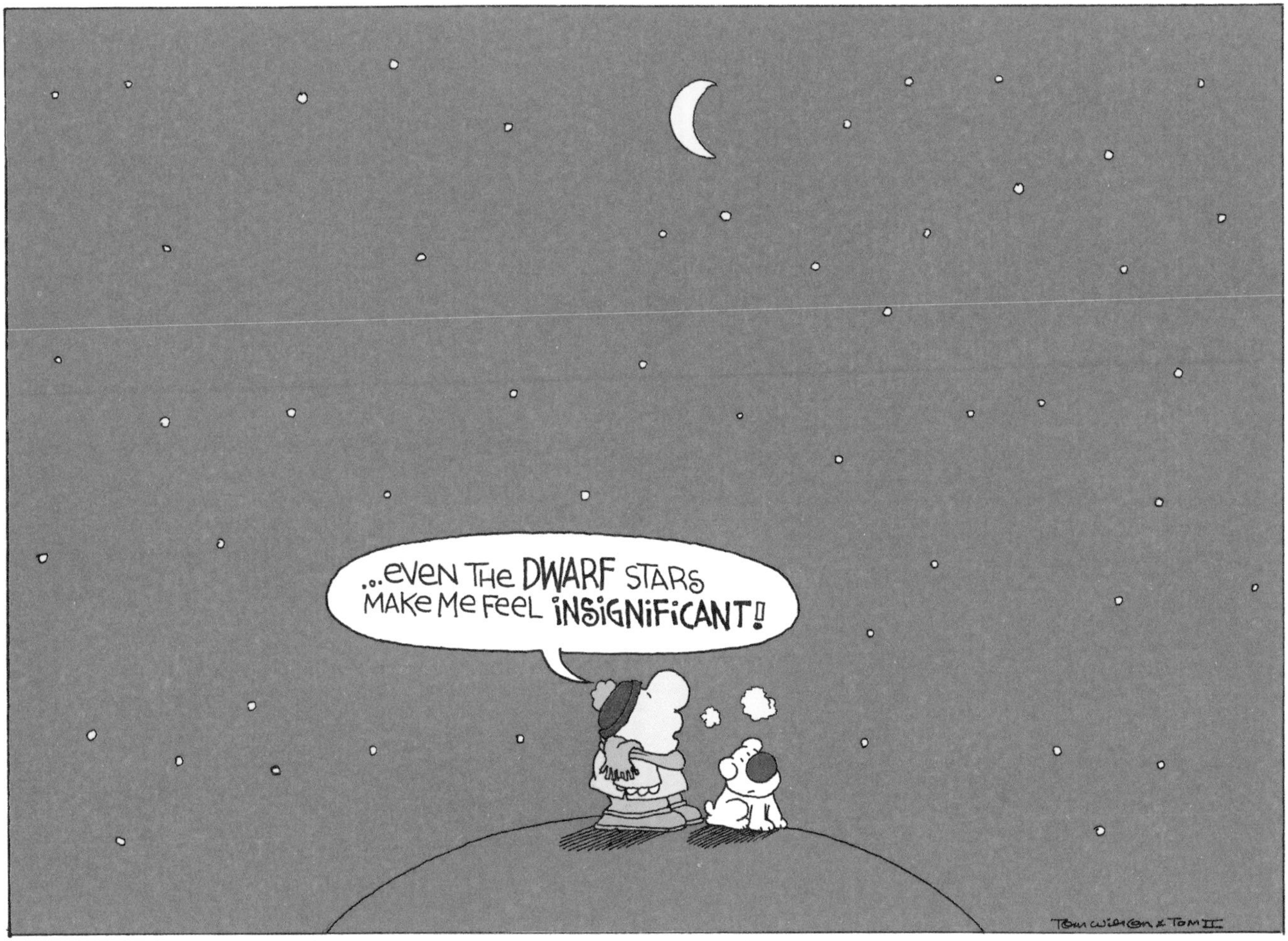
...EVEN THE DWARF STARS MAKE ME FEEL INSIGNIFICANT!
TOM WILSON & TOM II

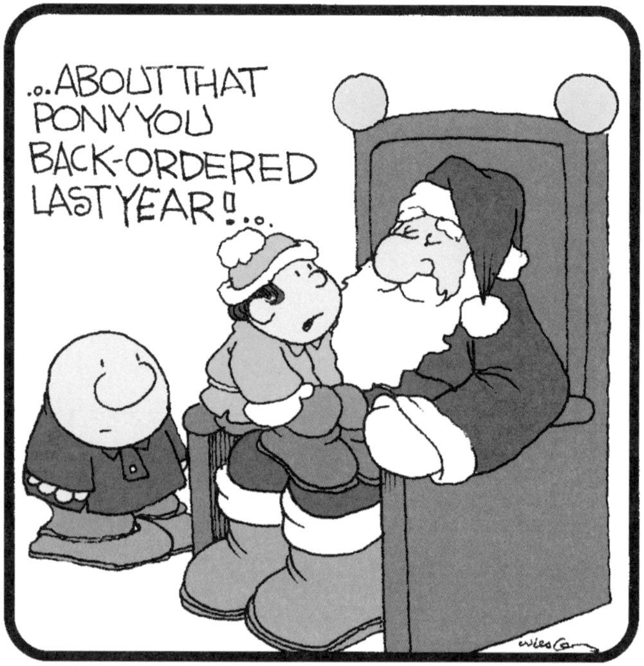
..o..ABOUT THAT PONY YOU BACK-ORDERED LAST YEAR!..o.

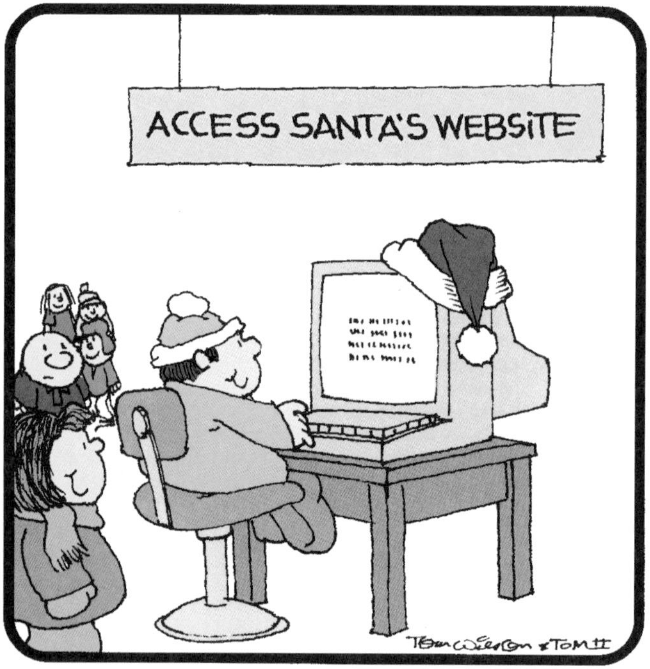
ACCESS SANTA'S WEBSITE

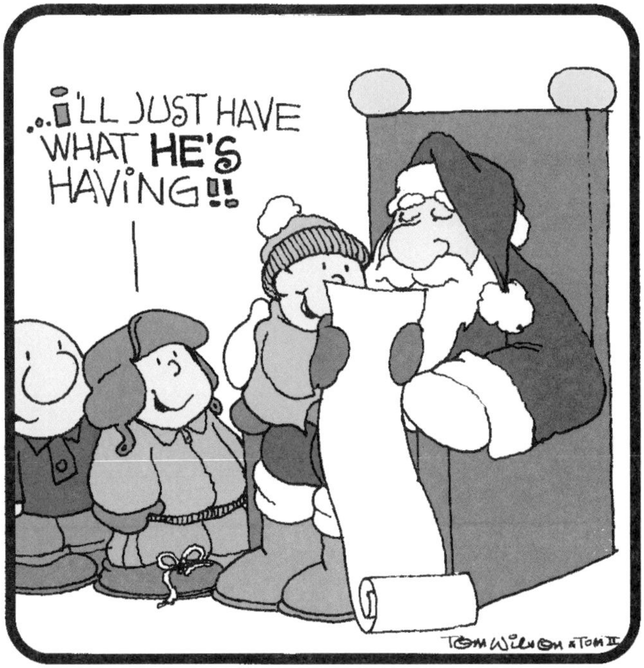
..I'LL JUST HAVE WHAT HE'S HAVING!!
TOM WILSON & TOM II

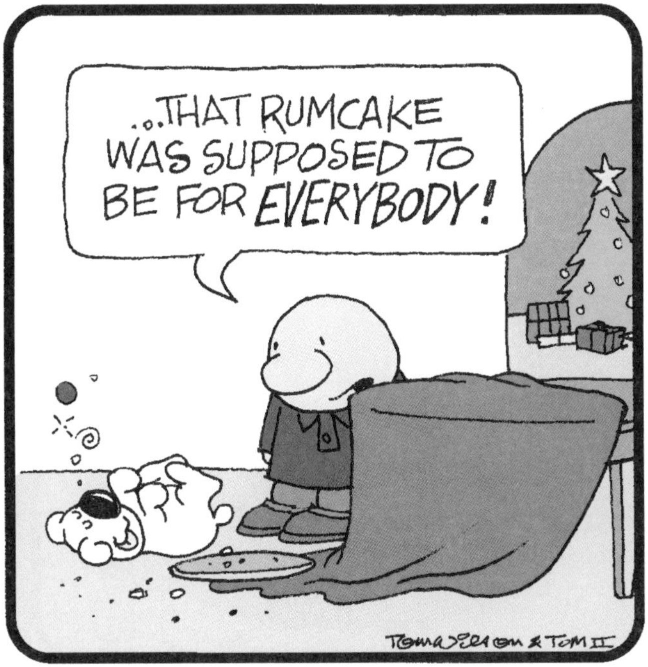
...THAT RUMCAKE WAS SUPPOSED TO BE FOR EVERYBODY!
TOM WILSON & TOM II

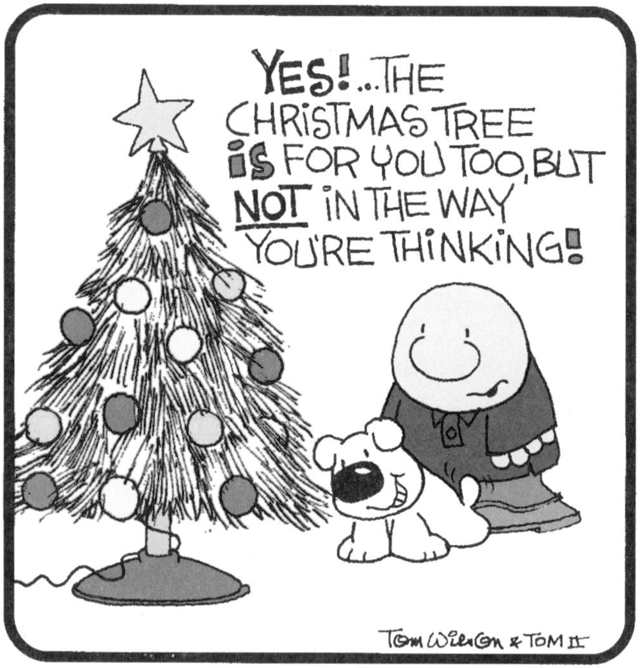
YES!...THE CHRISTMAS TREE IS FOR YOU TOO, BUT NOT IN THE WAY YOU'RE THINKING!
TOM WILSON & TOM II

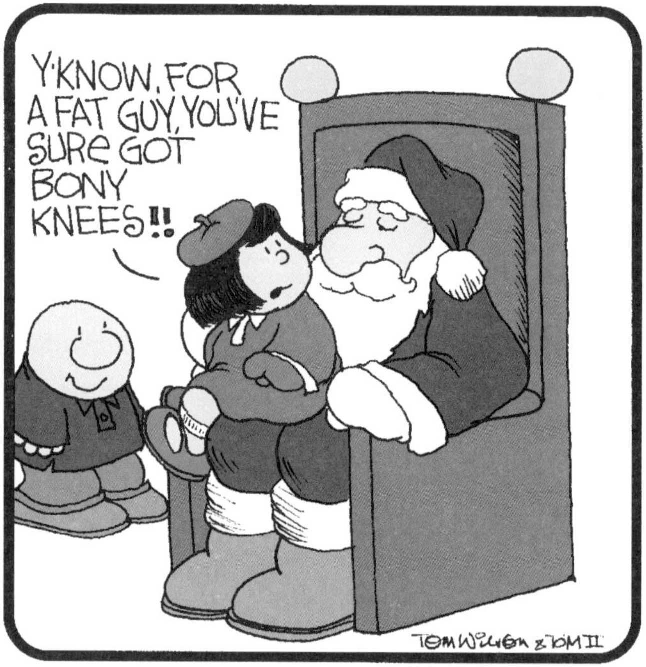
Y'KNOW, FOR A FAT GUY, YOU'VE SURE GOT BONY KNEES!!
TOM WILSON & TOM II

..YOUR LOBSTER SURPRISE, SIR!
PSSSSST!
..YOU GONNA EAT THOSE FRIES?
...I NEVER WOULD'VE FIGURED YOU FOR THE LOBSTER...YOU LOOK MORE LIKE THE 'SHRIMP'! TO ME... HEH, HEH
..NEXT TIME CHECK OUT THE DIET PLATE, LARD-BOTTOM!
THIS IS YOUR LAST WARNING, FRANÇOIS...KNOCK OFF THE VENTRILOQUIST ACT!!

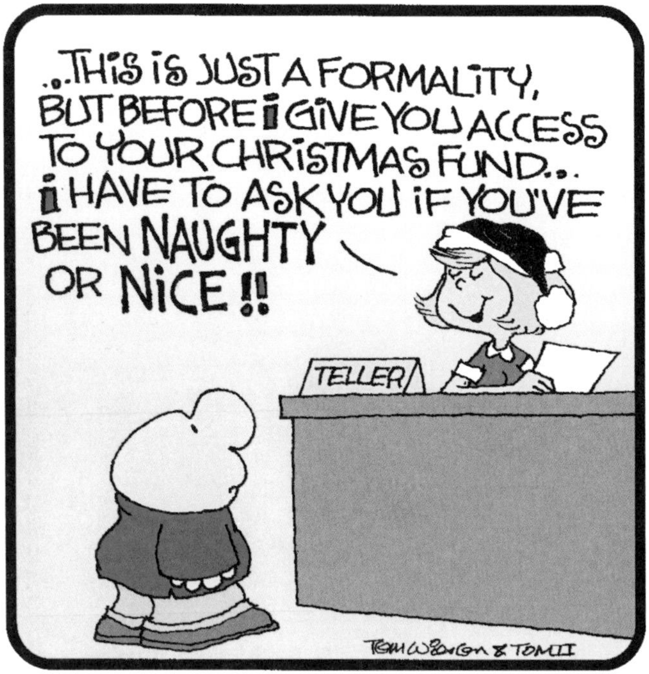
..THIS IS JUST A FORMALITY, BUT BEFORE I GIVE YOU ACCESS TO YOUR CHRISTMAS FUND... I HAVE TO ASK YOU IF YOU'VE BEEN NAUGHTY OR NICE !!
TELLER
TOM WILSON & TOM II

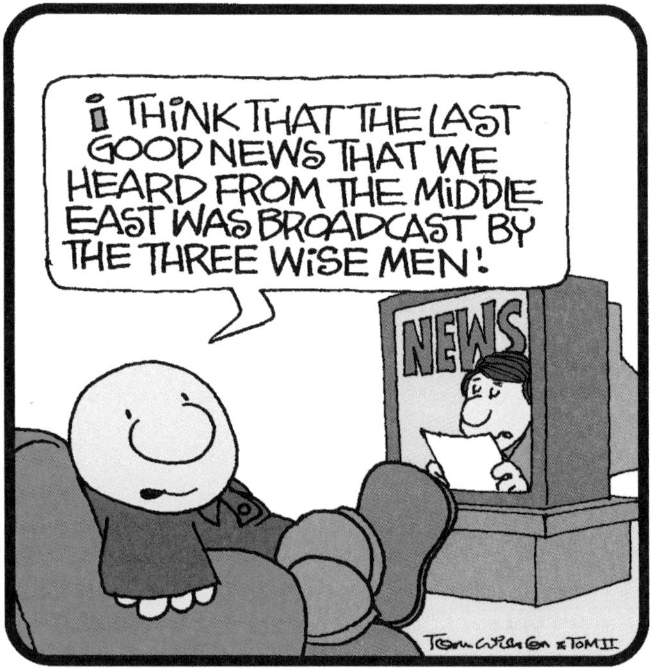
I THINK THAT THE LAST GOOD NEWS THAT WE HEARD FROM THE MIDDLE EAST WAS BROADCAST BY THE THREE WISE MEN!
NEWS
TOM WILSON & TOM II

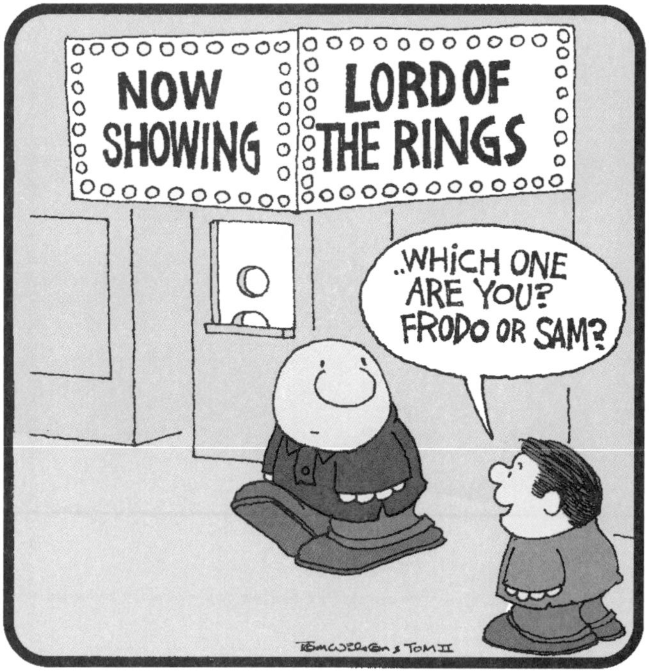
NOW SHOWING
LORD OF THE RINGS
..WHICH ONE ARE YOU? FRODO OR SAM?

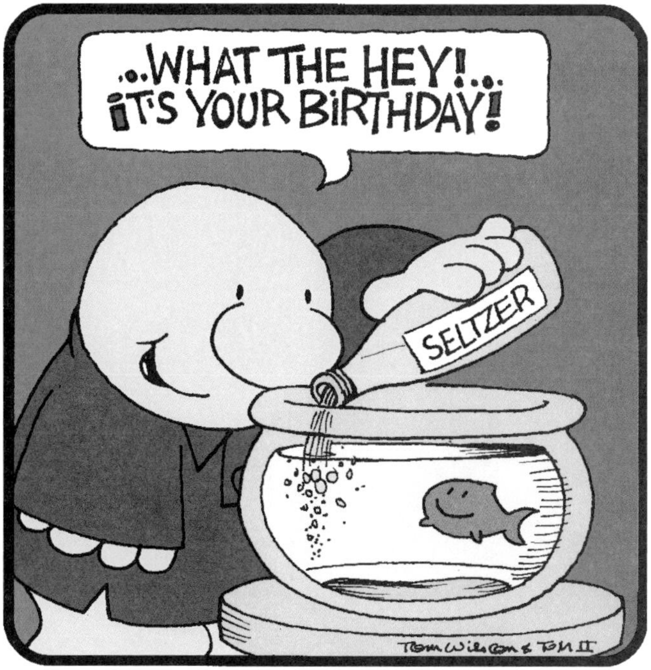
..WHAT THE HEY!.. IT'S YOUR BIRTHDAY!
SELTZER

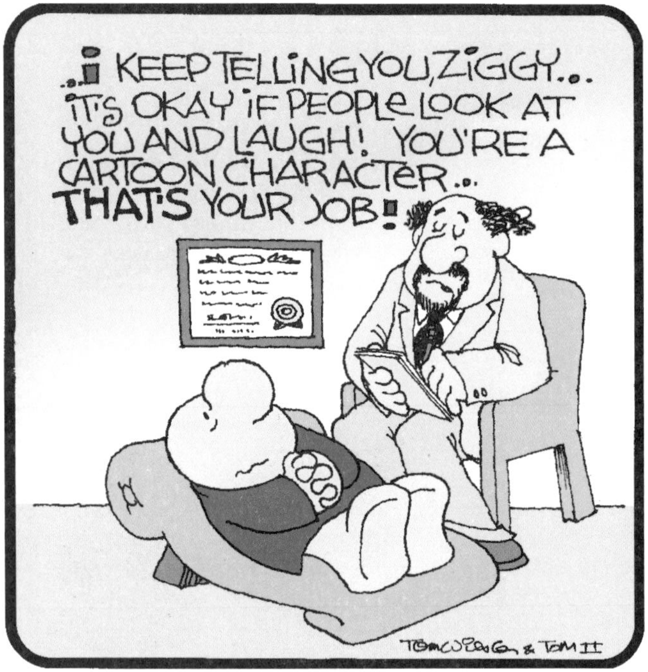
..I KEEP TELLING YOU, ZIGGY... IT'S OKAY IF PEOPLE LOOK AT YOU AND LAUGH! YOU'RE A CARTOON CHARACTER... THAT'S YOUR JOB!
TOM WILSON & TOM II

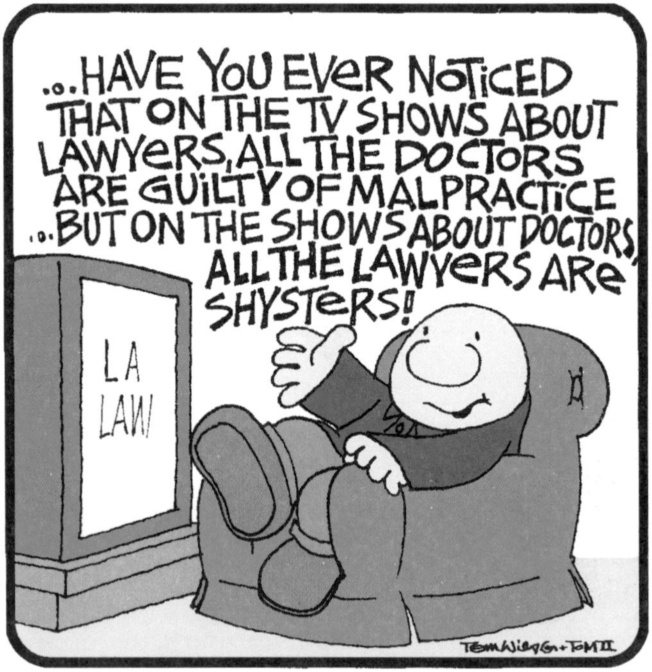
...HAVE YOU EVER NOTICED THAT ON THE TV SHOWS ABOUT LAWYERS, ALL THE DOCTORS ARE GUILTY OF MALPRACTICE ...BUT ON THE SHOWS ABOUT DOCTORS, ALL THE LAWYERS ARE SHYSTERS!
LA LAW
TOM WILSON + TOM II

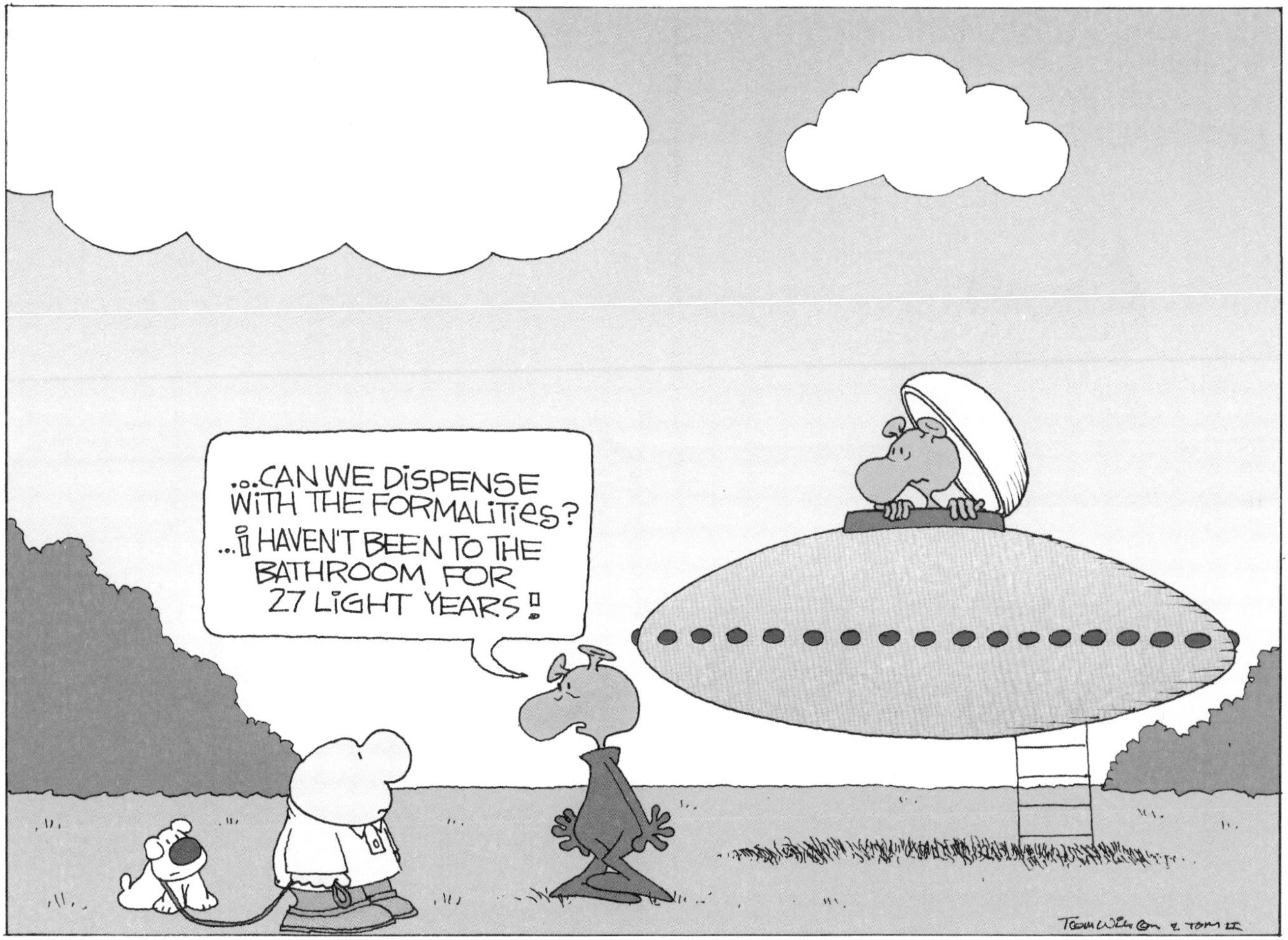

...CAN WE DISPENSE WITH THE FORMALITIES? ...I HAVEN'T BEEN TO THE BATHROOM FOR 27 LIGHT YEARS!

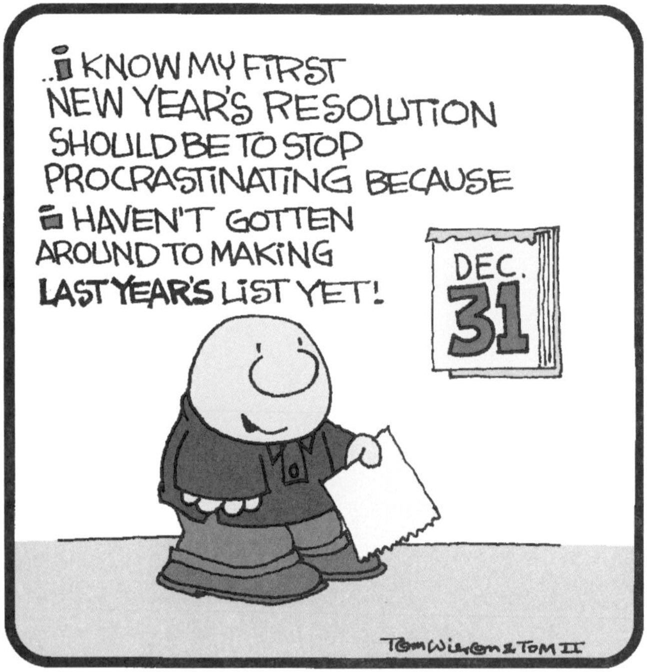
..I KNOW MY FIRST NEW YEAR'S RESOLUTION SHOULD BE TO STOP PROCRASTINATING BECAUSE I HAVEN'T GOTTEN AROUND TO MAKING LAST YEAR'S LIST YET!
DEC. 31
TOM WILSON & TOM II

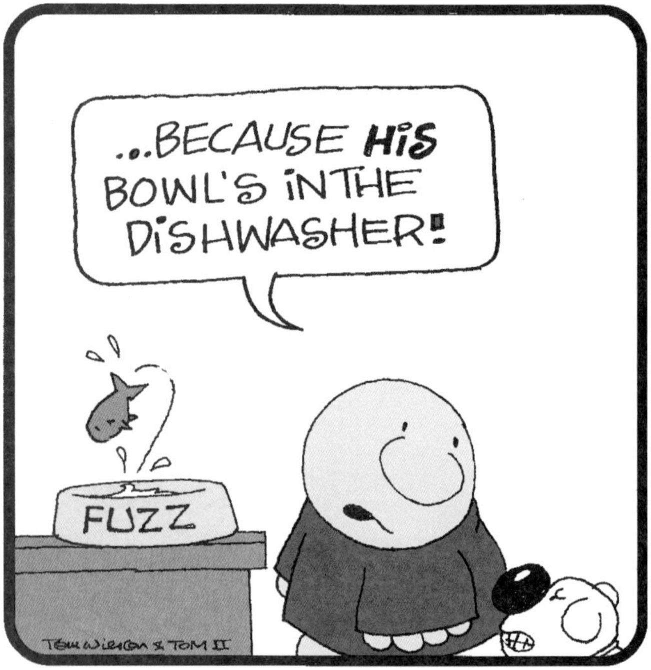
...BECAUSE HIS BOWL'S IN THE DISHWASHER!
FUZZ
TOM WILSON & TOM II

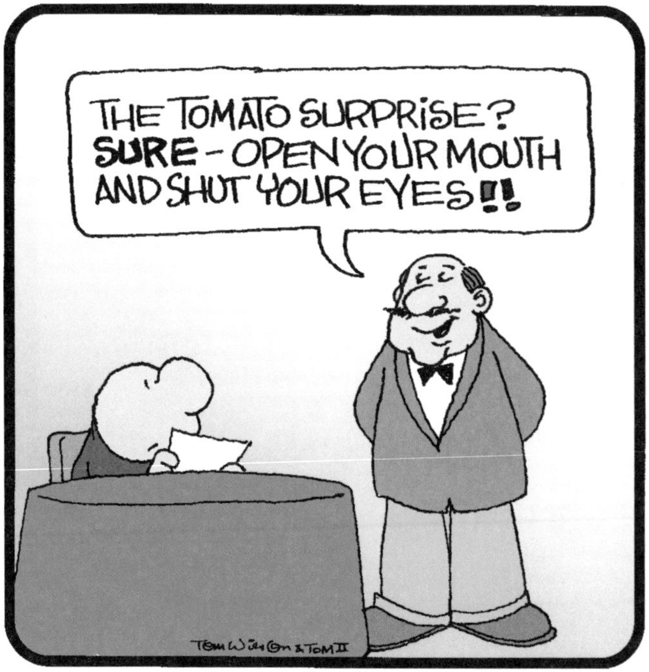
THE TOMATO SURPRISE? SURE - OPEN YOUR MOUTH AND SHUT YOUR EYES!!
TOM WILSON & TOM II

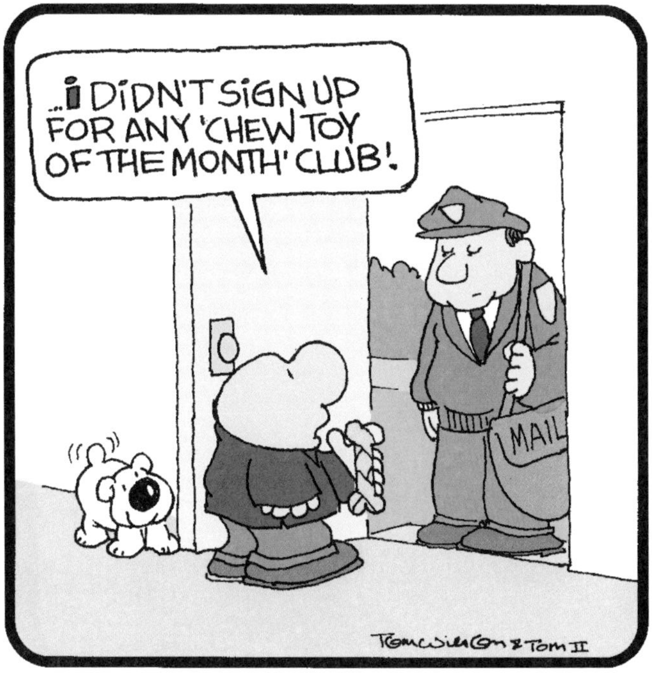
...I DIDN'T SIGN UP FOR ANY 'CHEW TOY OF THE MONTH' CLUB!
MAIL
TOM WILSON & TOM II

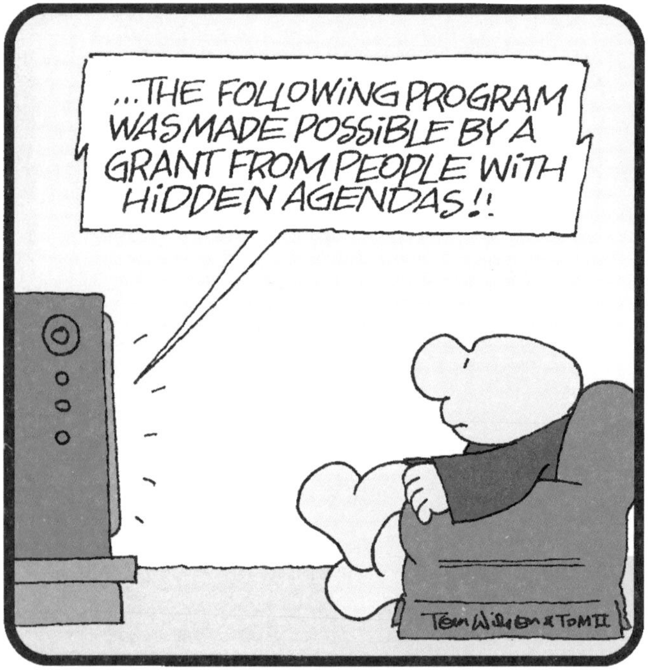
...THE FOLLOWING PROGRAM WAS MADE POSSIBLE BY A GRANT FROM PEOPLE WITH HIDDEN AGENDAS!!
Tom Wilson & TOM II

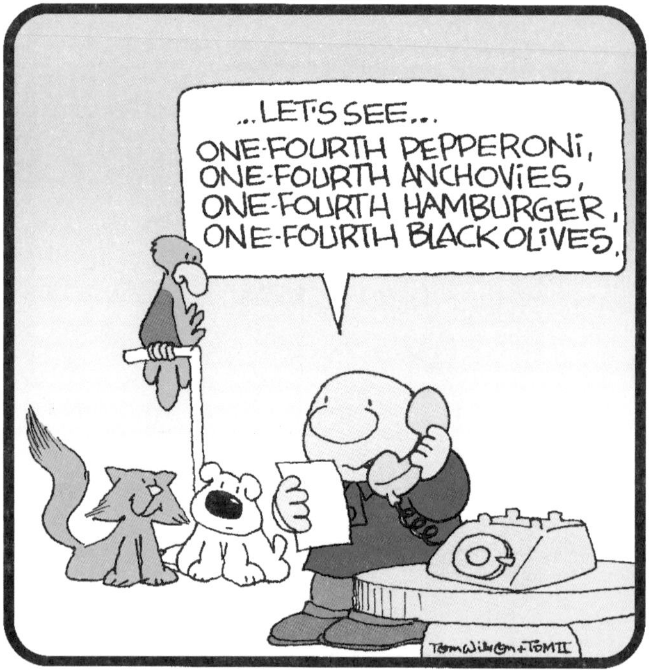
...LET'S SEE... ONE-FOURTH PEPPERONI, ONE-FOURTH ANCHOVIES, ONE-FOURTH HAMBURGER, ONE-FOURTH BLACK OLIVES,
Tom Wilson + TOM II

STARLIGHT...STARBRIGHT I WISH I MAY... I WISH I MIGHT...
I WISH I HAD GREAT WISDOM!!
...WHO AM I KIDDING? WISDOM ISN'T SOMETHING YOU GET BY WISHING FOR IT!!
...IT'S SOMETHING YOU HAVE TO EARN WITH YEARS OF EXPERIENCE!
...AS WELL AS LOTS OF MATURITY AND PATIENCE AND...SAY!!
...MAYBE THAT WISH WORKED AFTER ALL!!

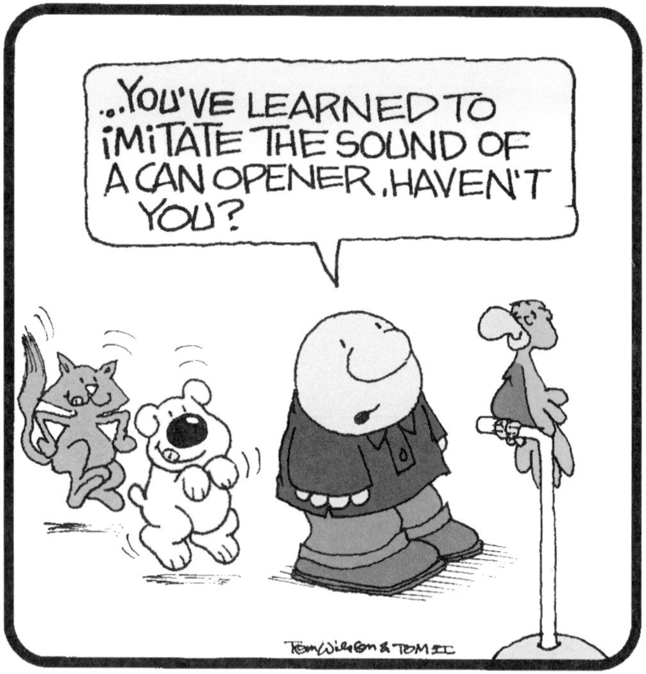
..YOU'VE LEARNED TO IMITATE THE SOUND OF A CAN OPENER, HAVEN'T YOU?
TOM WILSON & TOM II

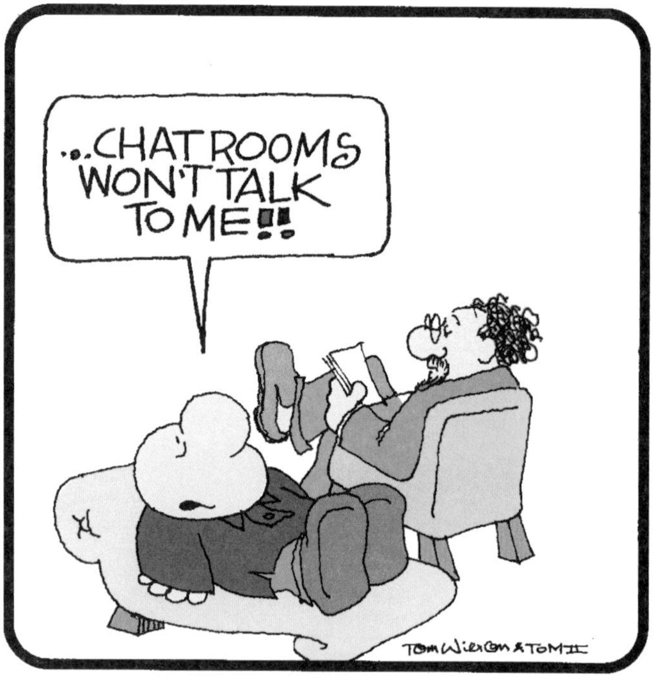
..CHAT ROOMS WON'T TALK TO ME!!
TOM WILSON & TOM II

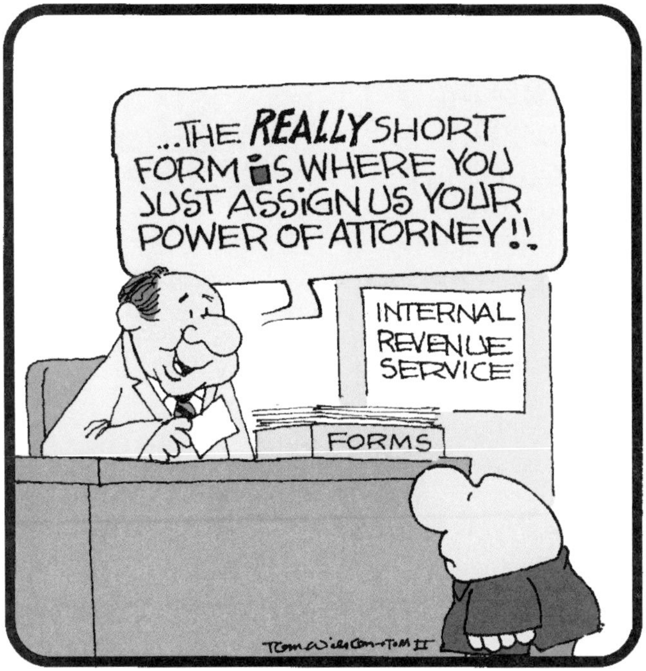
...THE REALLY SHORT FORM IS WHERE YOU JUST ASSIGN US YOUR POWER OF ATTORNEY!!
INTERNAL REVENUE SERVICE
FORMS

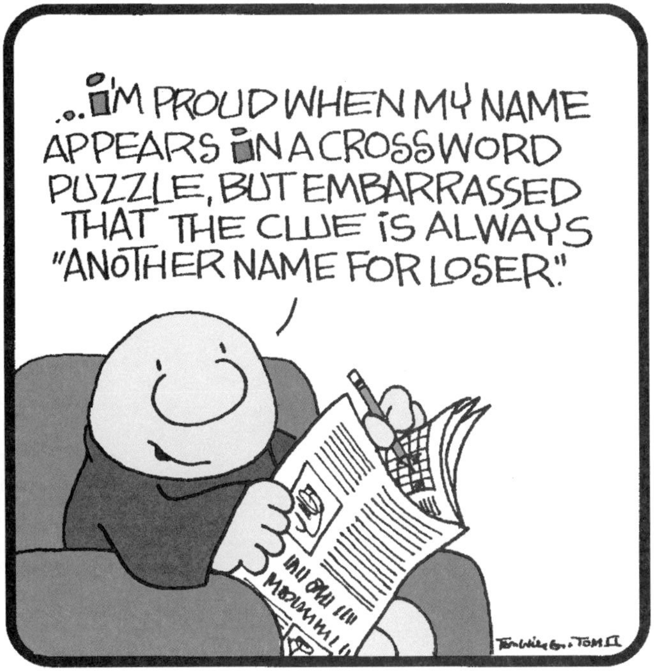
...I'M PROUD WHEN MY NAME APPEARS IN A CROSSWORD PUZZLE, BUT EMBARRASSED THAT THE CLUE IS ALWAYS "ANOTHER NAME FOR LOSER."

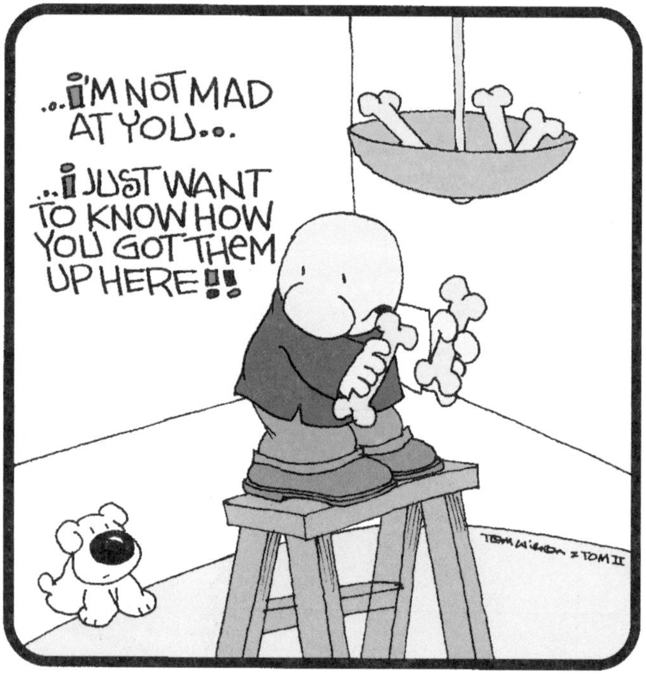
..I'M NOT MAD AT YOU...
..I JUST WANT TO KNOW HOW YOU GOT THEM UP HERE!!

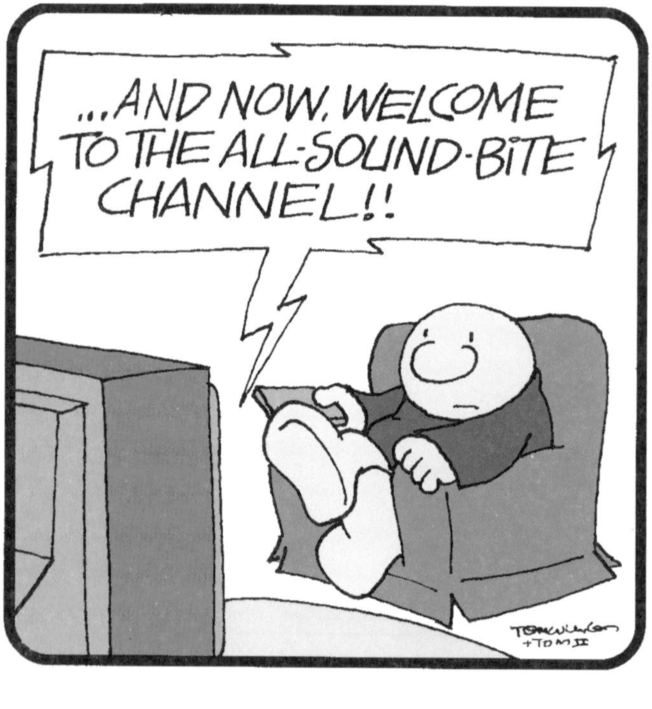
...AND NOW, WELCOME TO THE ALL-SOUND-BITE CHANNEL!!

HEY! A LETTER FROM THE I.R.S. MAYBE IT'S MY TAX REFUND.

DEAR MR. ZIGGY: WE'RE SURE THAT YOU, LIKE ALL AMERICANS, HAVE BEEN ANTICIPATING YOUR TAX-CUT REBATE.

UNFORTUNATELY, THERE WAS A SLIGHT MISCALCULATION IN THE FUNDS SET ASIDE FOR THIS PURPOSE!

AS THE DISBURSEMENTS HAVE BEEN MADE IN ALPHABETICAL ORDER...

...AND SINCE YOUR NAME BEGINS WITH THE THE LETTER 'Z'...

..WE HOPE THAT YOU'LL ENJOY THE ENCLOSED COUPONS FOR $300 IN FREE OIL LUBES!

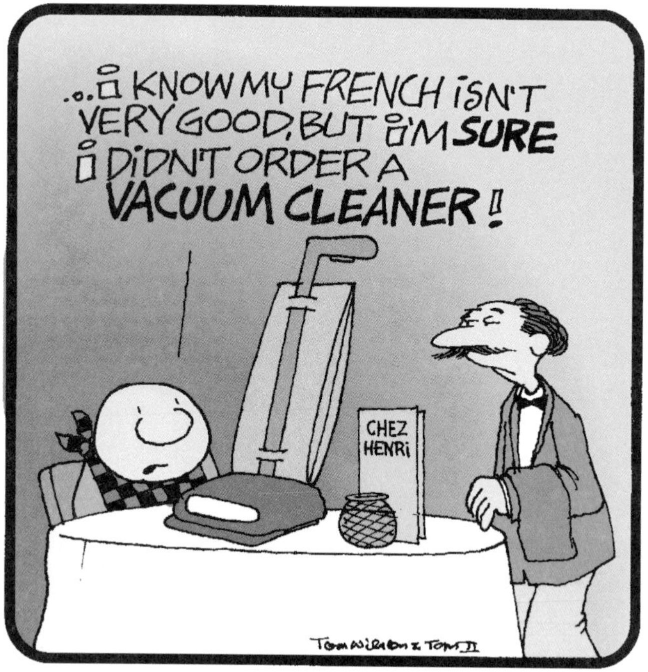
...I KNOW MY FRENCH ISN'T VERY GOOD, BUT I'M SURE I DIDN'T ORDER A VACUUM CLEANER!
CHEZ HENRI

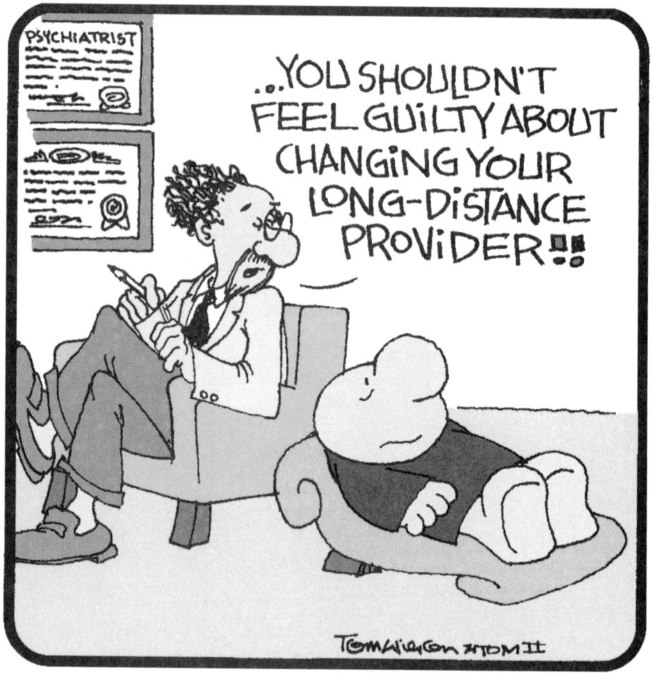
PSYCHIATRIST
...YOU SHOULDN'T FEEL GUILTY ABOUT CHANGING YOUR LONG-DISTANCE PROVIDER!!!

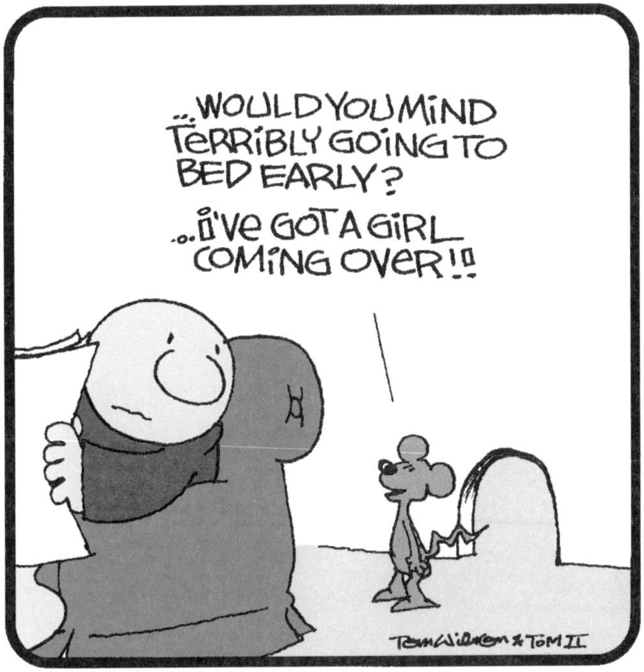
..WOULD YOU MIND TERRIBLY GOING TO BED EARLY?
..I'VE GOT A GIRL COMING OVER!!
TOM WILSON & TOM II

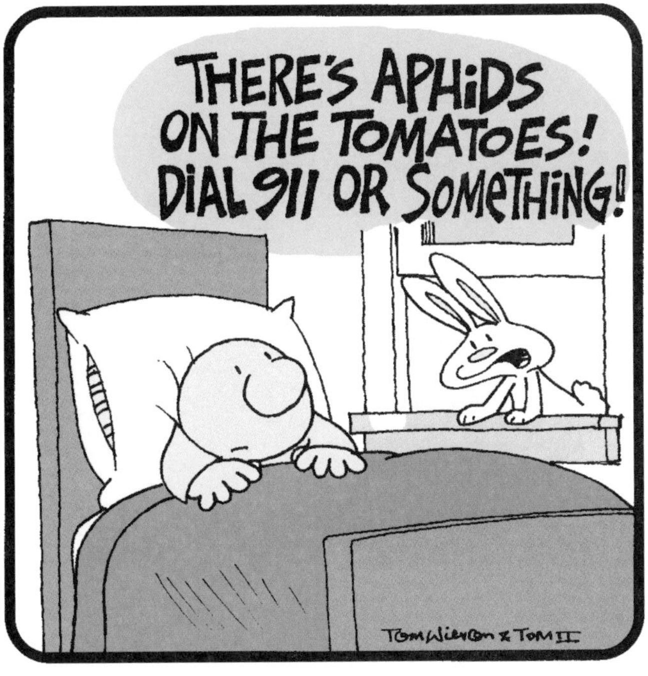
THERE'S APHIDS ON THE TOMATOES! DIAL 911 OR SOMETHING!
TOM WILSON & TOM II

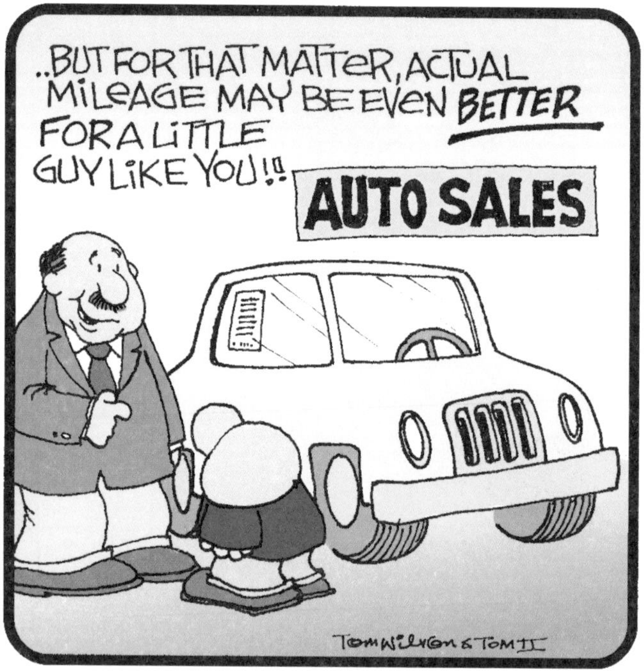
..BUT FOR THAT MATTER, ACTUAL MILEAGE MAY BE EVEN BETTER FOR A LITTLE GUY LIKE YOU!!
AUTO SALES
TOM WILSON & TOM II

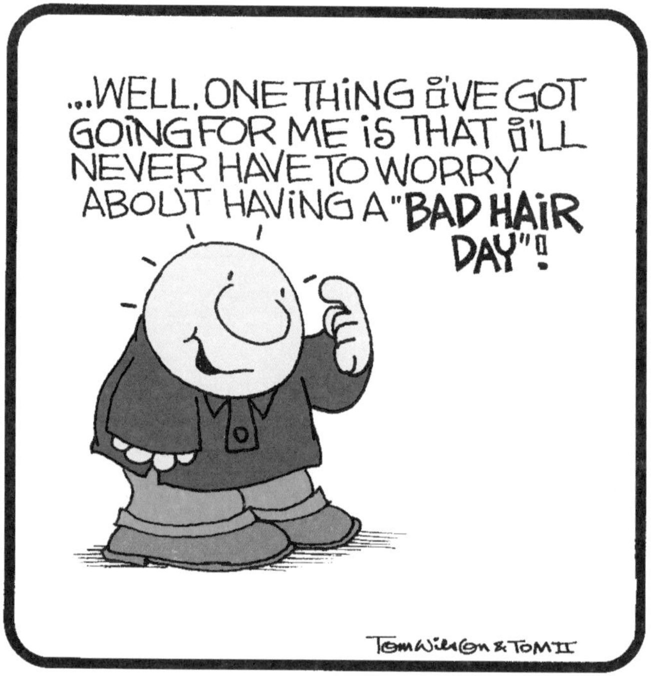
...WELL, ONE THING I'VE GOT GOING FOR ME IS THAT I'LL NEVER HAVE TO WORRY ABOUT HAVING A "BAD HAIR DAY"!
TOM WILSON & TOM II

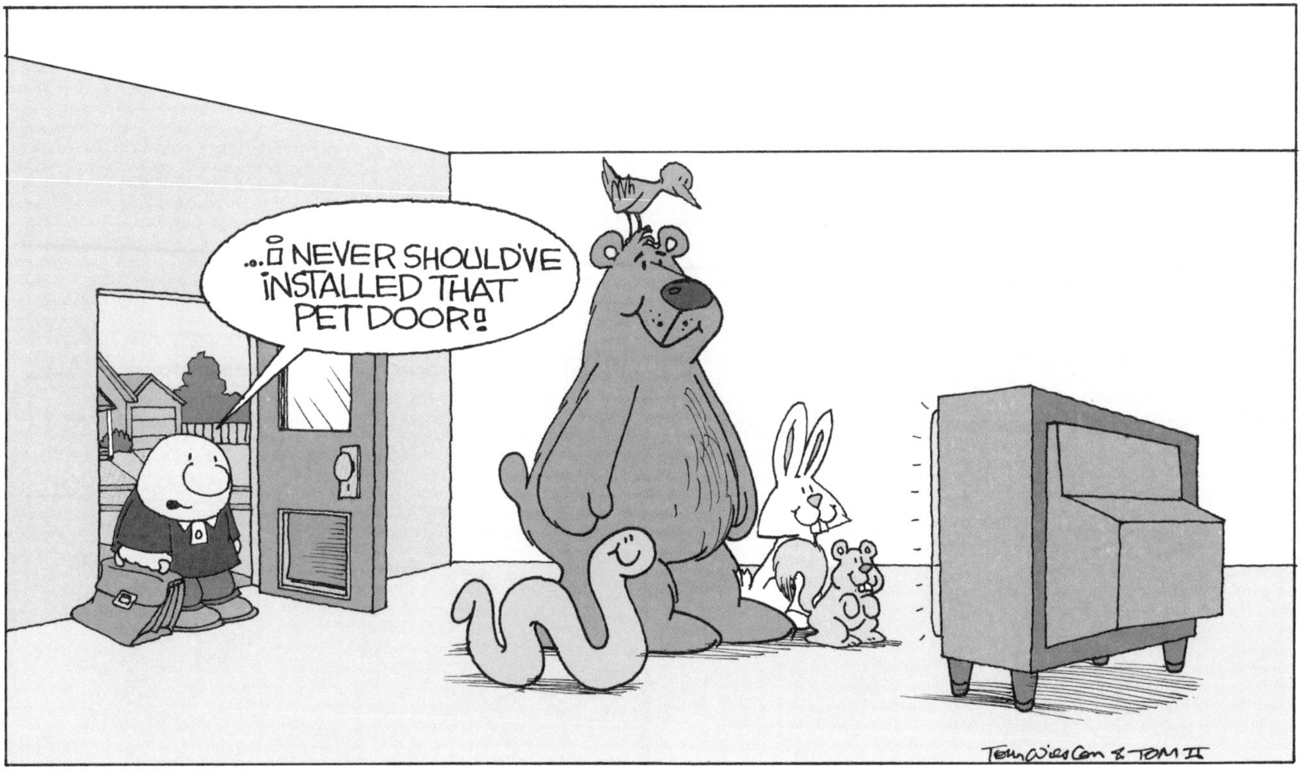
...I NEVER SHOULD'VE INSTALLED THAT PET DOOR!
Tom Wilson & Tom II

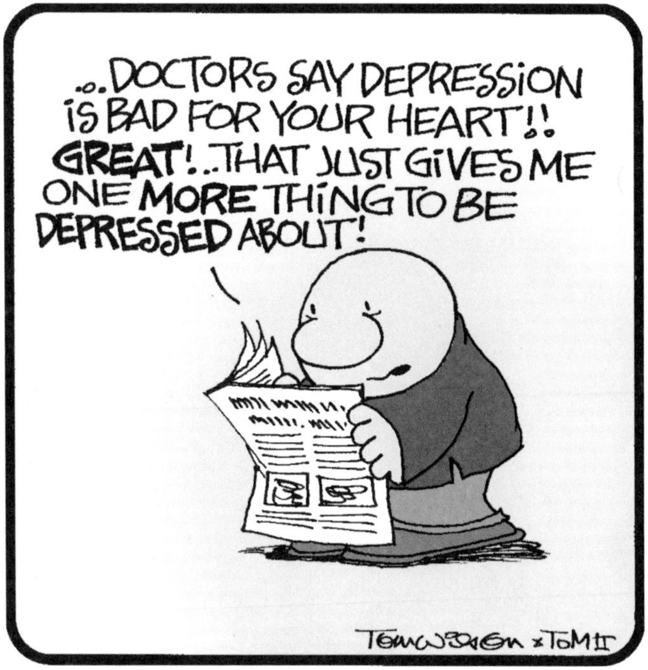
..DOCTORS SAY DEPRESSION IS BAD FOR YOUR HEART!! **GREAT!**..THAT JUST GIVES ME ONE **MORE** THING TO BE **DEPRESSED** ABOUT!
TOM WILSON & TOM II

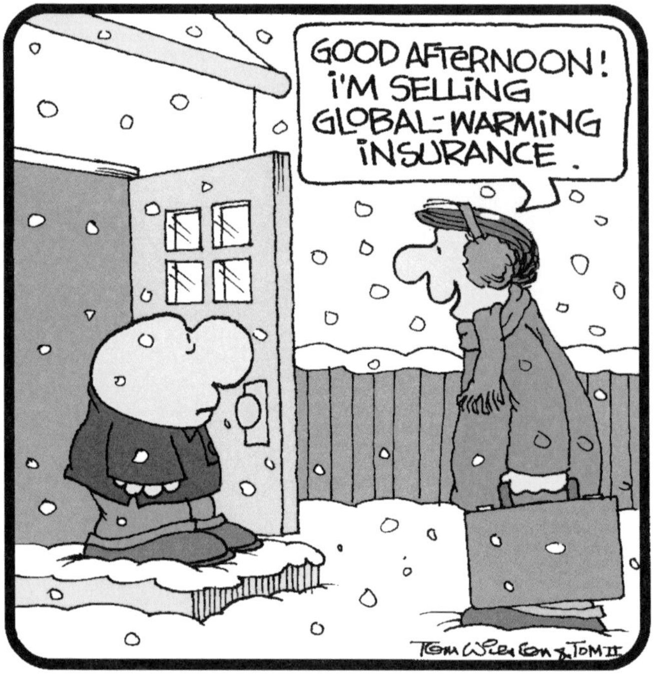
GOOD AFTERNOON! I'M SELLING GLOBAL-WARMING INSURANCE.
TOM WILSON & TOM II

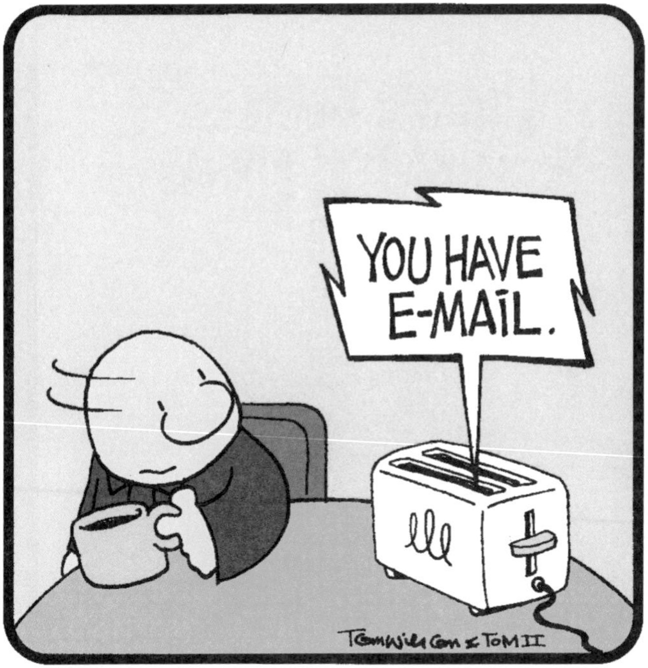
YOU HAVE E-MAIL.
TOM WILSON & TOM II

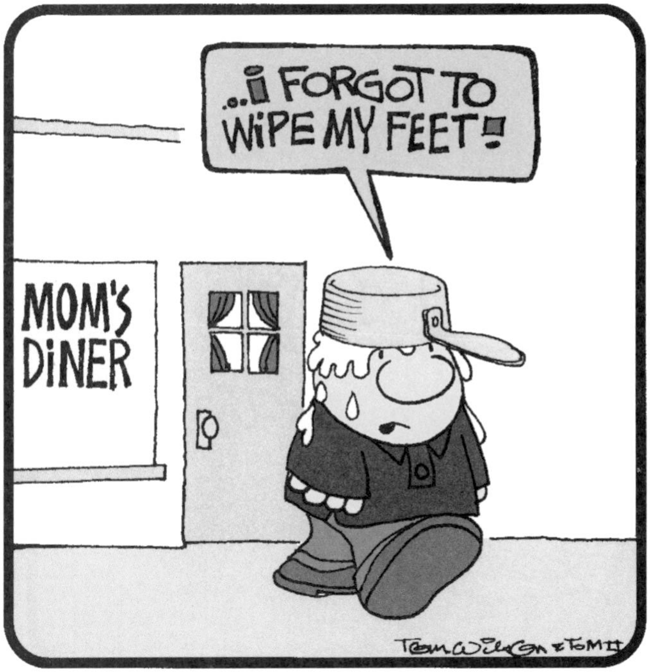
..I FORGOT TO WIPE MY FEET!!
MOM'S DINER
TOM WILSON & TOM II

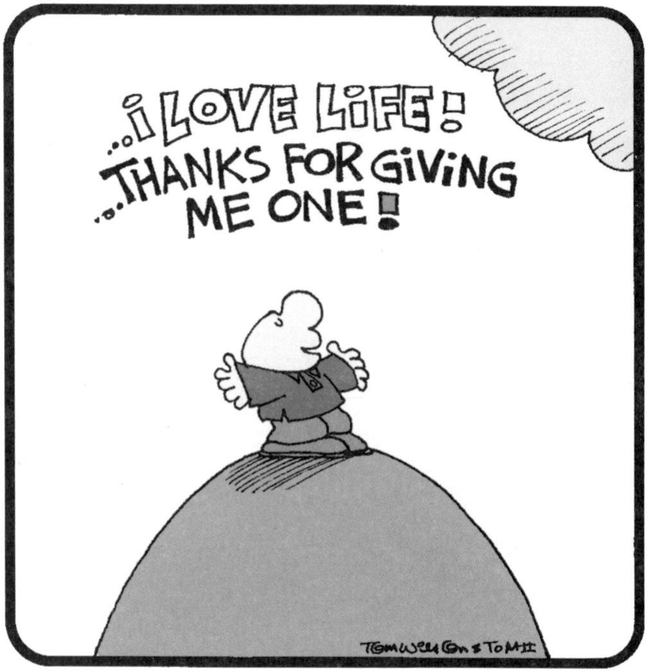
..I LOVE LIFE!
..THANKS FOR GIVING ME ONE!
TOM WILSON & TOM II

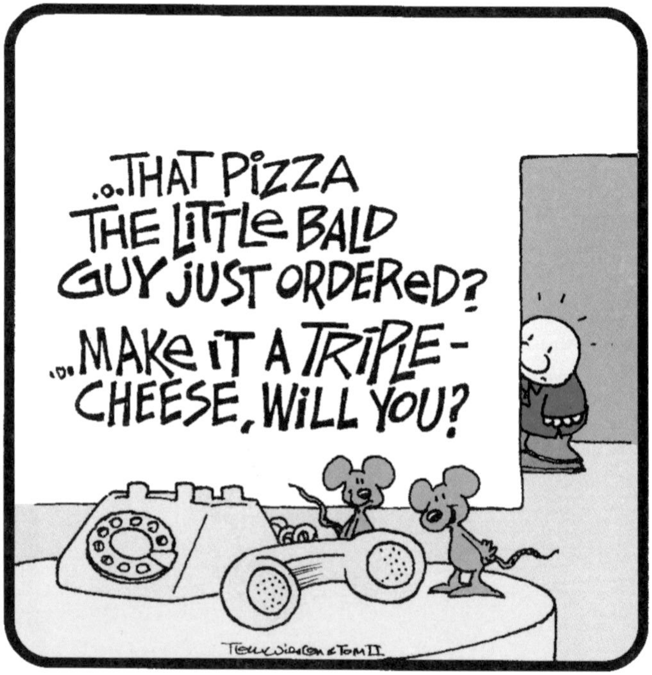
..THAT PIZZA THE LITTLE BALD GUY JUST ORDERED?
..MAKE IT A TRIPLE-CHEESE, WILL YOU?
TOM WILSON & TOM II

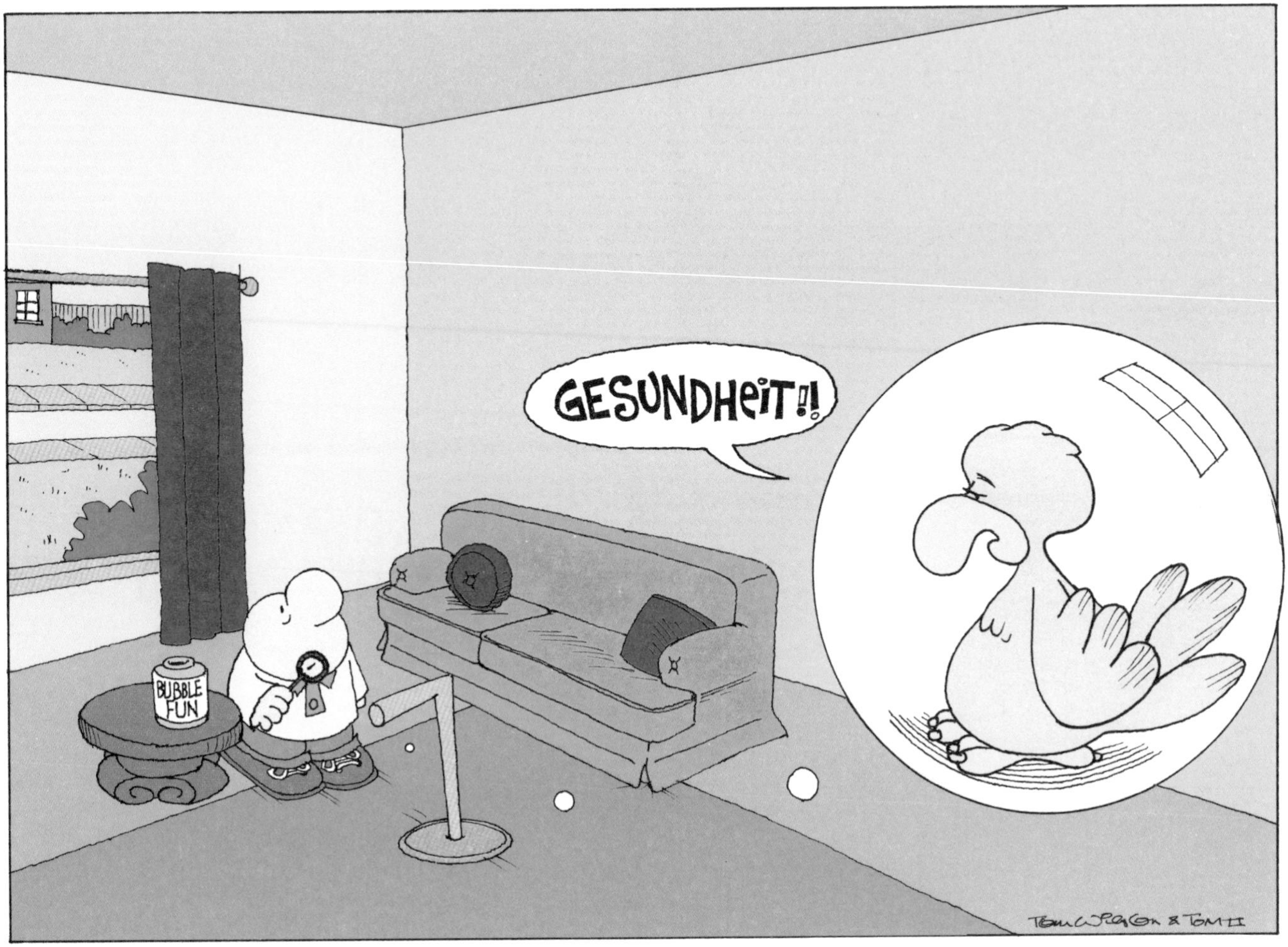
GESUNDHEIT!!
BUBBLE FUN
TOM WILSON & TOM II

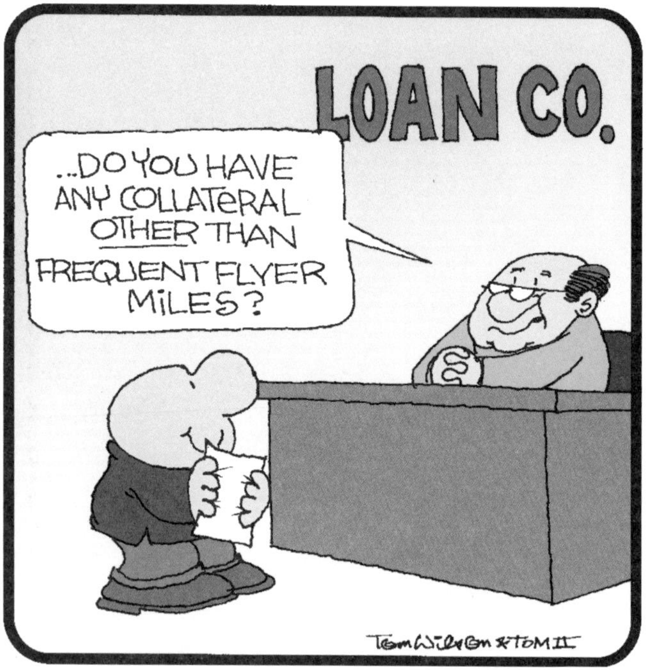
LOAN CO.
...DO YOU HAVE ANY COLLATERAL OTHER THAN FREQUENT FLYER MILES?
Tom Wilson & TOM II

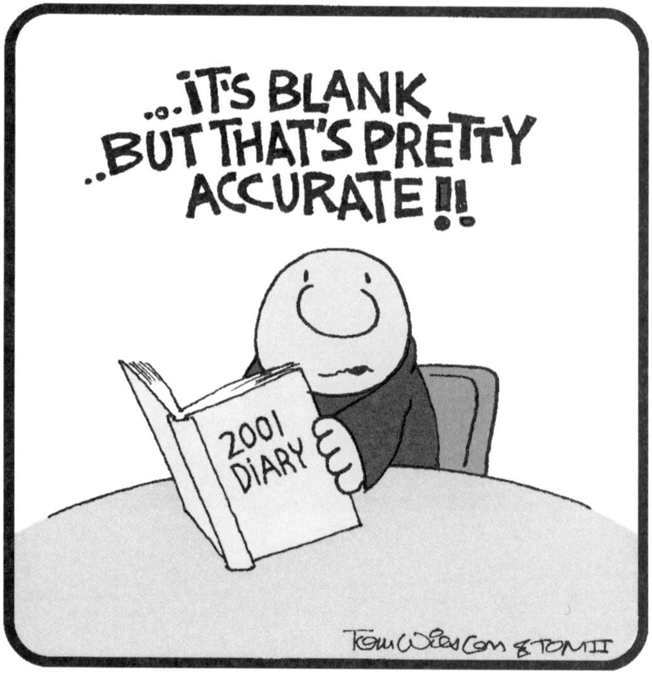
...IT'S BLANK ..BUT THAT'S PRETTY ACCURATE!!
2001 DIARY
Tom Wilson & TOM II

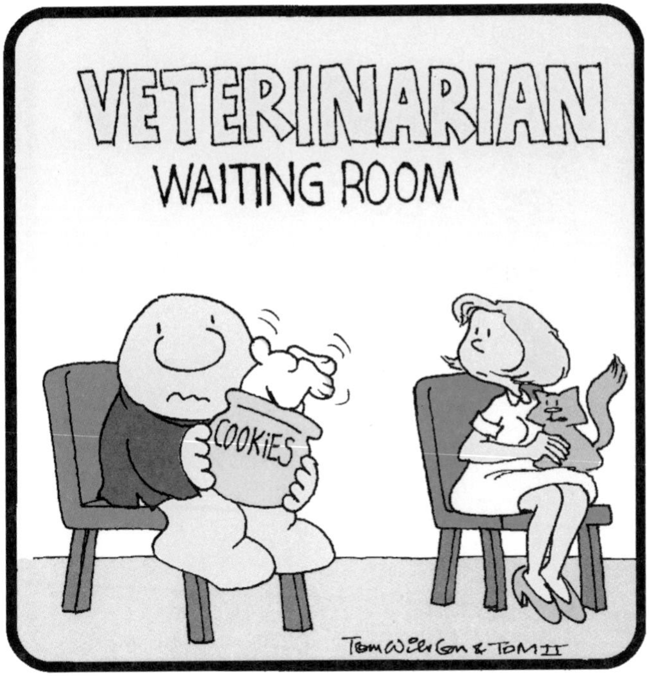
VETERINARIAN
WAITING ROOM
COOKIES
Tom Wilson & Tom II

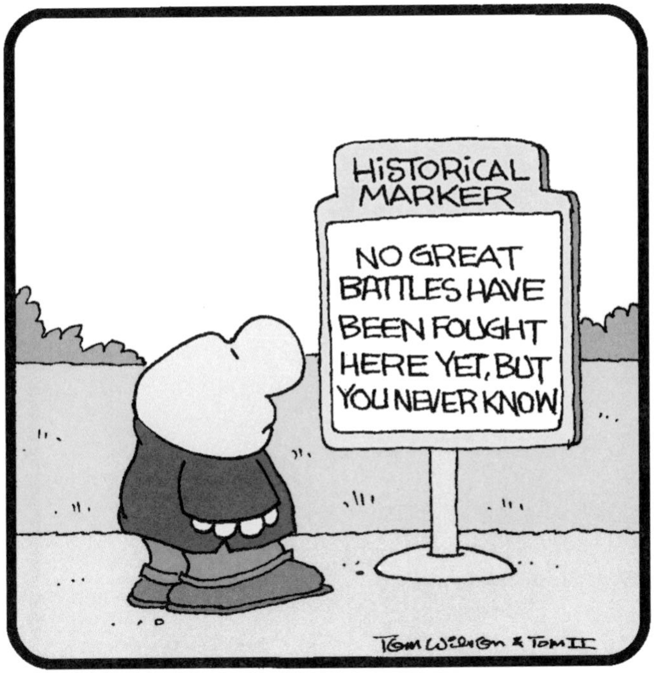
HISTORICAL MARKER
NO GREAT BATTLES HAVE BEEN FOUGHT HERE YET, BUT YOU NEVER KNOW
Tom Wilson & Tom II

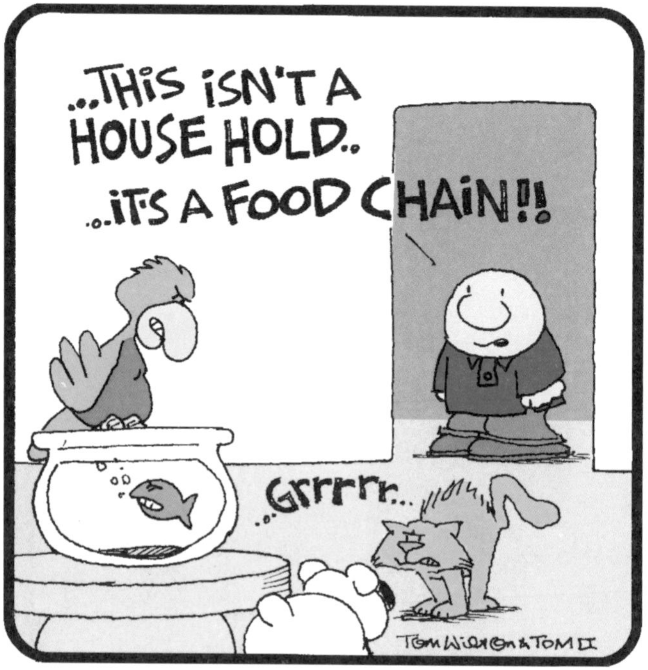
..THIS ISN'T A HOUSE HOLD..
..IT'S A FOOD CHAIN!!
..Grrrrr...
TOM WILSON & TOM II

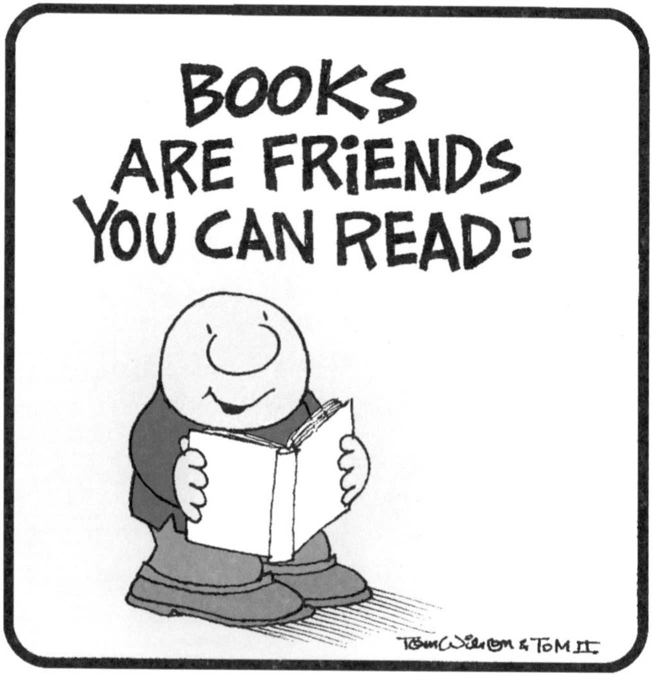
BOOKS ARE FRIENDS YOU CAN READ!
TOM WILSON & TOM II

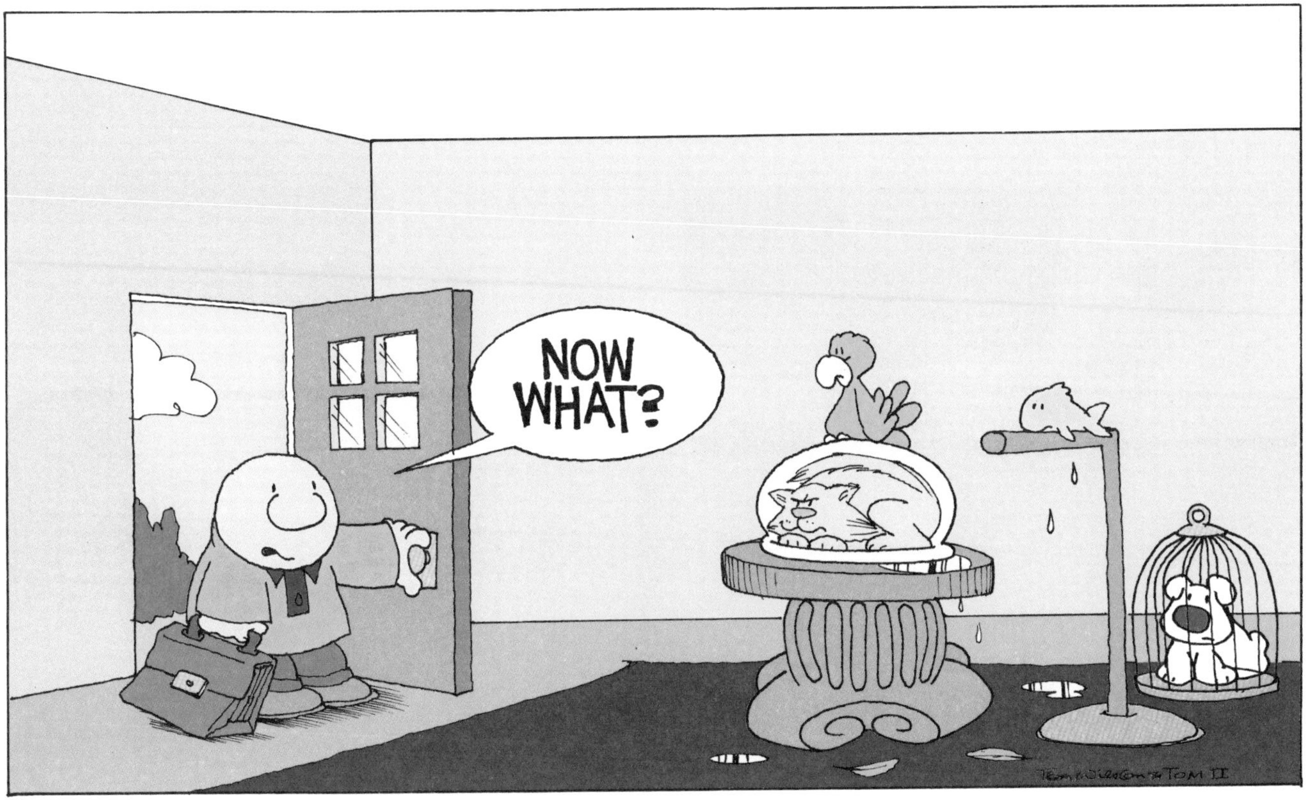
NOW WHAT?

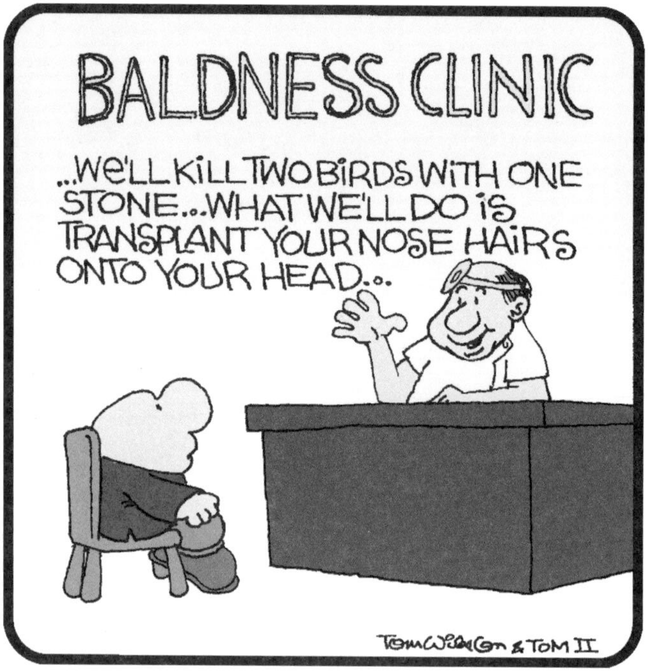
BALDNESS CLINIC
...WE'LL KILL TWO BIRDS WITH ONE STONE...WHAT WE'LL DO IS TRANSPLANT YOUR NOSE HAIRS ONTO YOUR HEAD...
Tom Wilson & TOM II

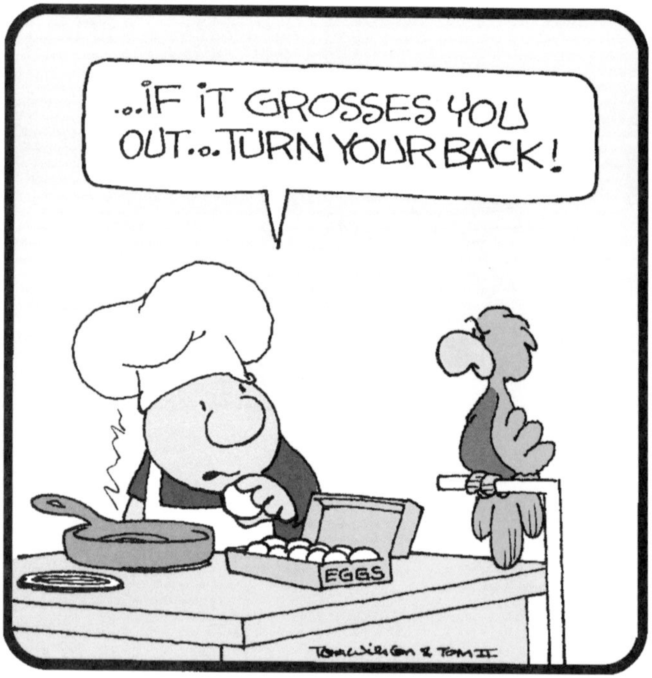
...IF IT GROSSES YOU OUT...TURN YOUR BACK!
EGGS
Tom Wilson & TOM II

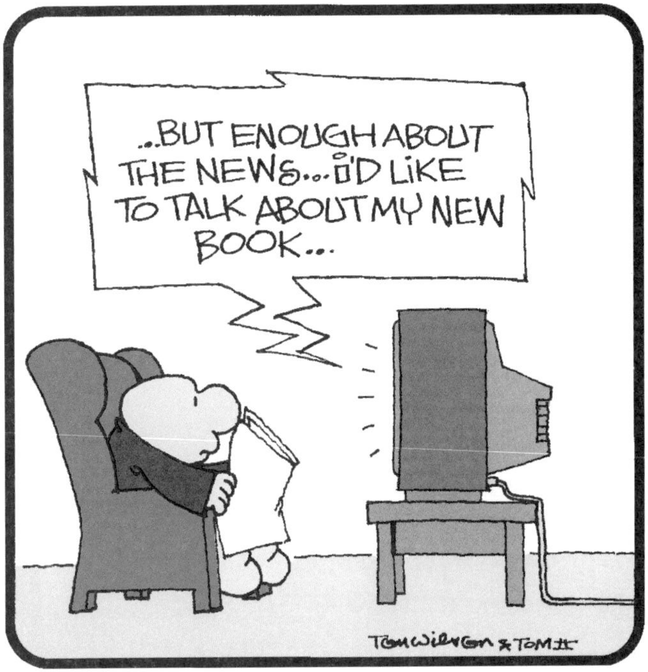
...BUT ENOUGH ABOUT THE NEWS...I'D LIKE TO TALK ABOUT MY NEW BOOK...
TOM WILSON & TOM II

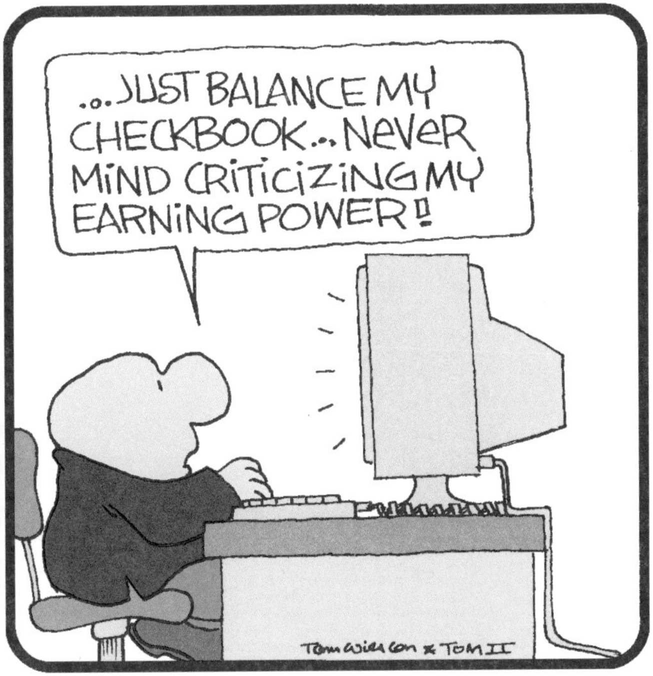
...JUST BALANCE MY CHECKBOOK... NEVER MIND CRITICIZING MY EARNING POWER!!
TOM WILSON & TOM II

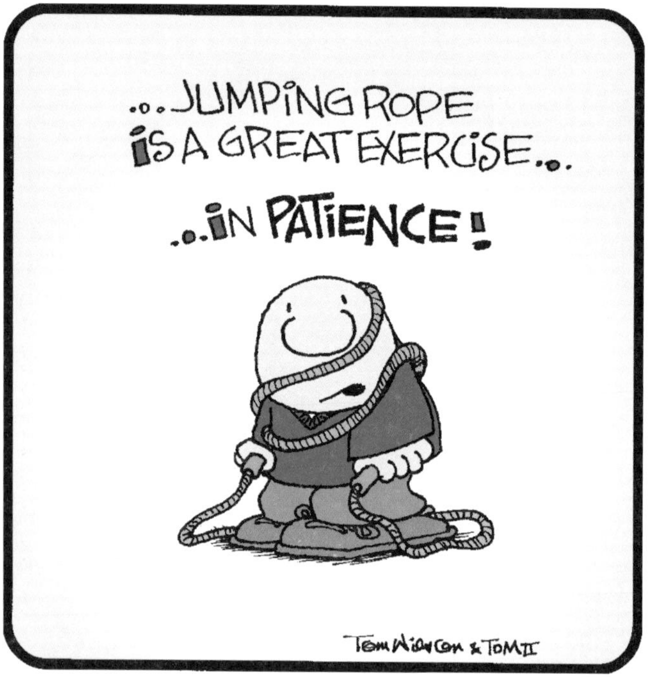
..JUMPING ROPE IS A GREAT EXERCISE...
...IN PATIENCE!
Tom Wilson & TOM II

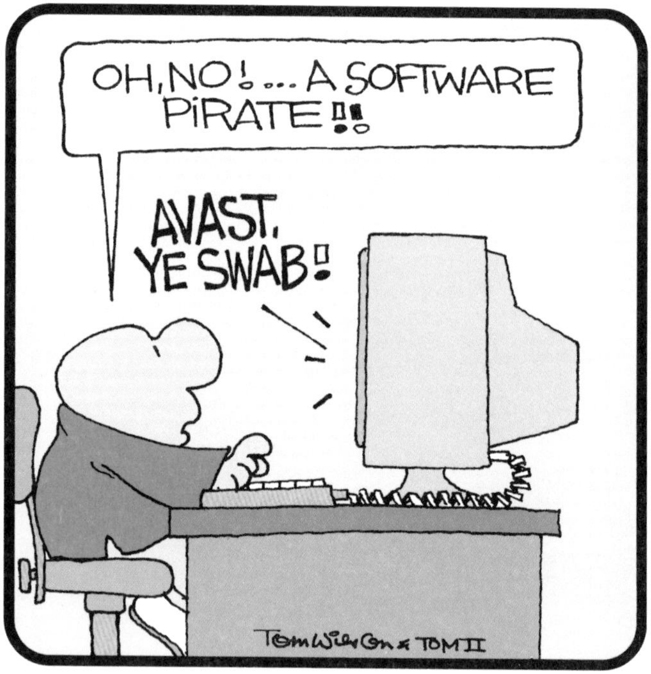
OH, NO!... A SOFTWARE PIRATE!!
AVAST, YE SWAB!
Tom Wilson & TOM II

...MY WHOLE LIFE JUST PASSED BEFORE MY EYES!
...AND IT WAS A "BLOOPER REEL"?!
TOM WILSON & TOM II

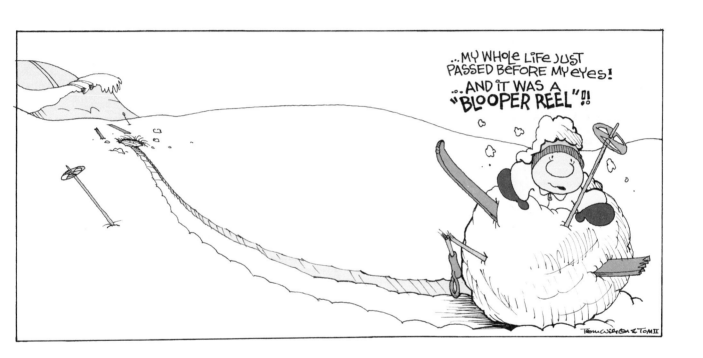

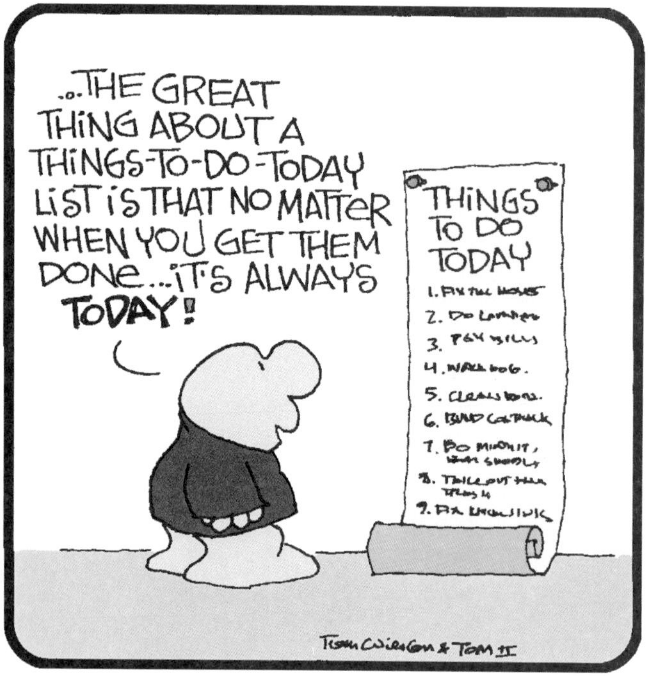
...THE GREAT THING ABOUT A THINGS-TO-DO-TODAY LIST IS THAT NO MATTER WHEN YOU GET THEM DONE...IT'S ALWAYS **TODAY**!
THINGS TO DO TODAY

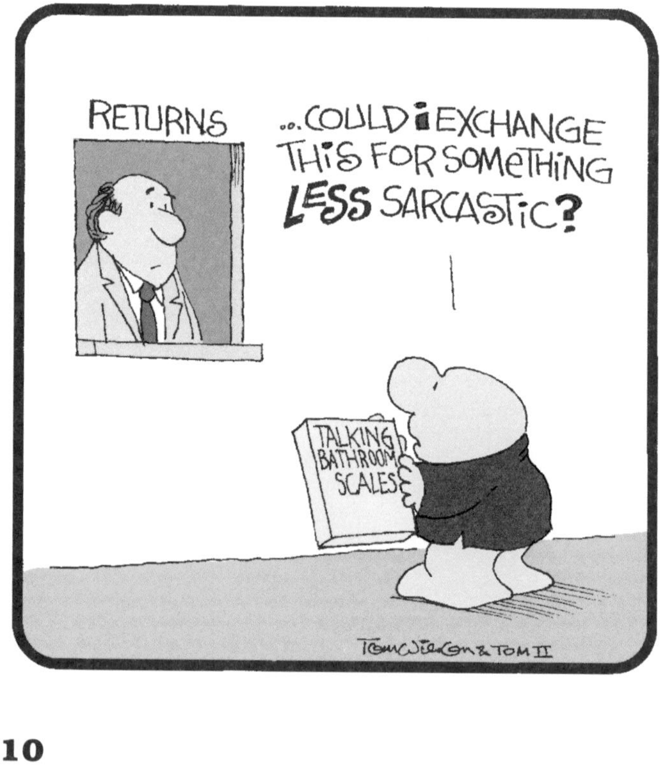
RETURNS
...COULD I EXCHANGE THIS FOR SOMETHING **LESS** SARCASTIC?
TALKING BATHROOM SCALES

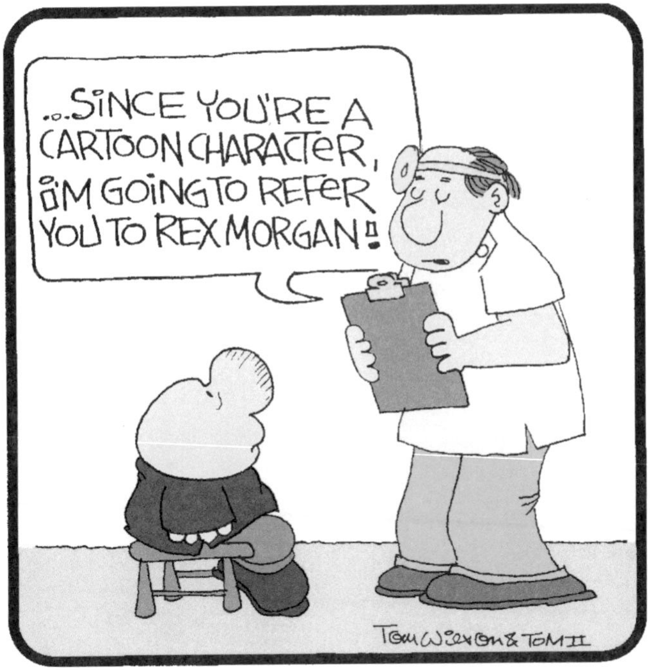
...SINCE YOU'RE A CARTOON CHARACTER, I'M GOING TO REFER YOU TO REX MORGAN!!
TOM WILSON & TOM II

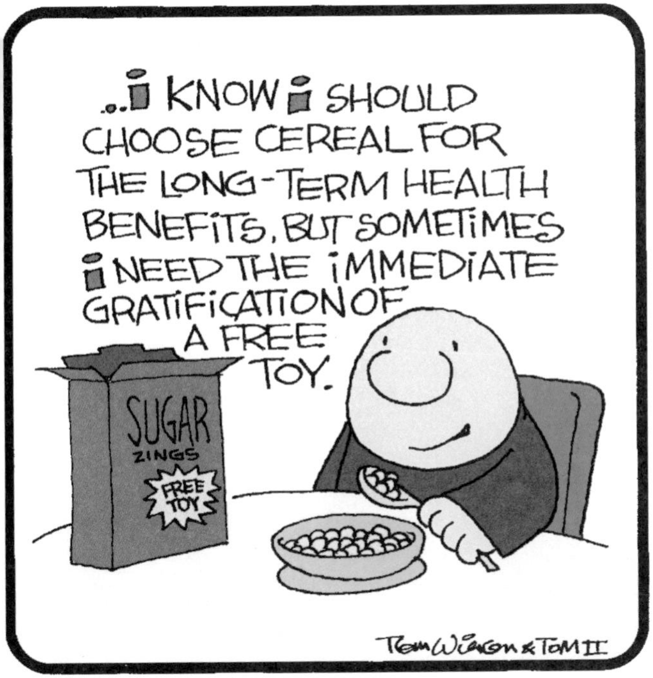
...I KNOW I SHOULD CHOOSE CEREAL FOR THE LONG-TERM HEALTH BENEFITS, BUT SOMETIMES I NEED THE IMMEDIATE GRATIFICATION OF A FREE TOY.
SUGAR ZINGS
FREE TOY
TOM WILSON & TOM II

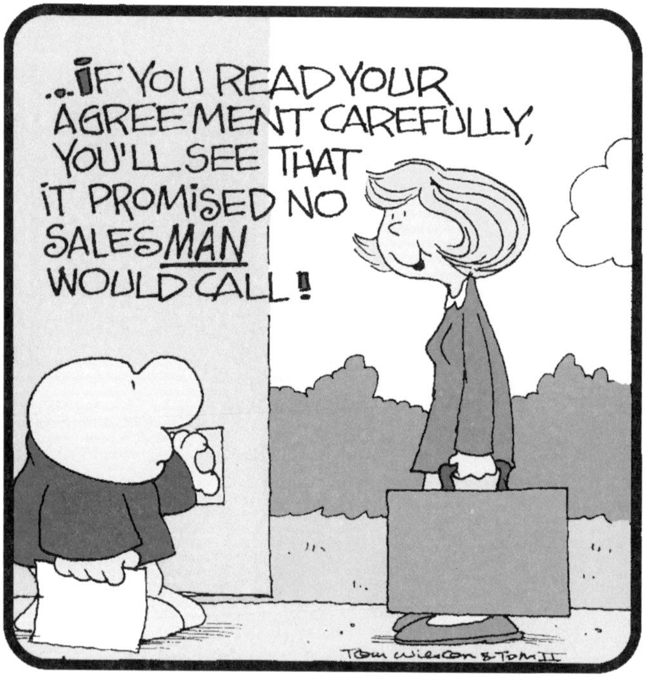
..IF YOU READ YOUR AGREEMENT CAREFULLY, YOU'LL SEE THAT IT PROMISED NO SALESMAN WOULD CALL!

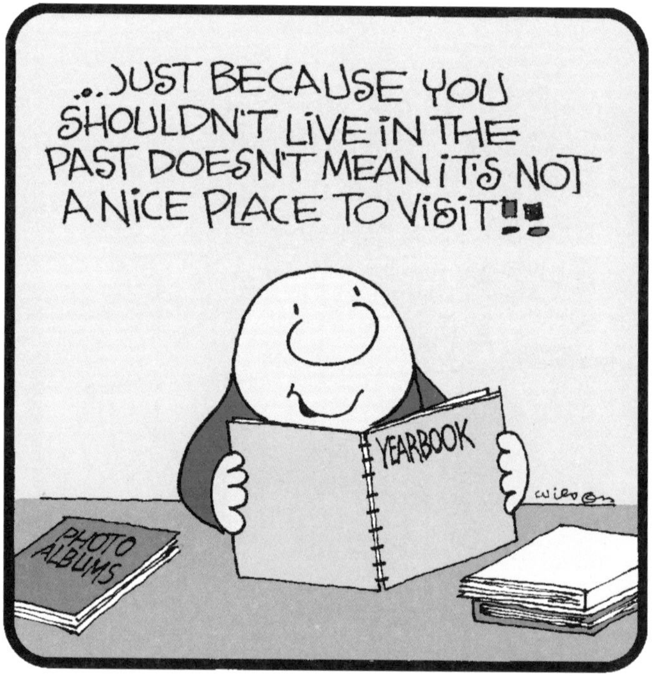
..JUST BECAUSE YOU SHOULDN'T LIVE IN THE PAST DOESN'T MEAN IT'S NOT A NICE PLACE TO VISIT!!
YEARBOOK
PHOTO ALBUMS

CARTOON SYNDICATE
...COULD WE GO BACK TO THE OLD FORMAT?
...I'M JUST NOT CUT OUT FOR AN ADVENTURE STRIP.
EDITOR

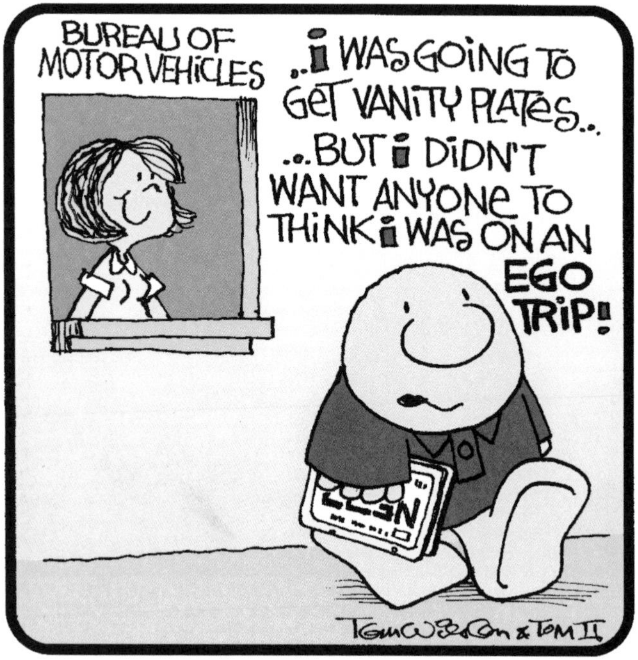
BUREAU OF MOTOR VEHICLES
..I WAS GOING TO GET VANITY PLATES..
..BUT I DIDN'T WANT ANYONE TO THINK I WAS ON AN EGO TRIP!

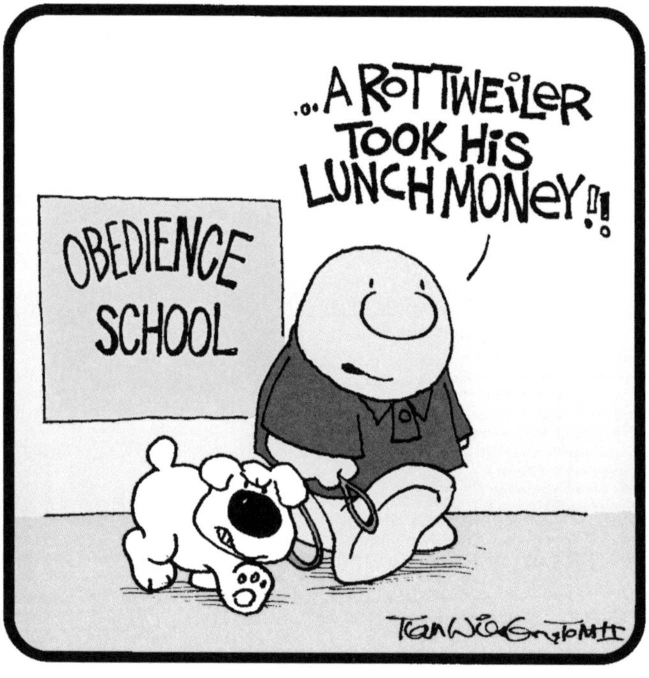
..A ROTTWEILER TOOK HIS LUNCH MONEY!!
OBEDIENCE SCHOOL

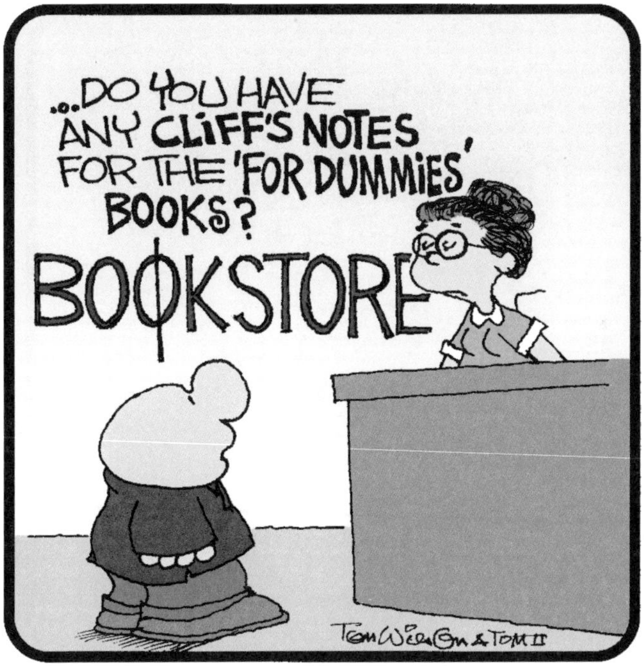
..DO YOU HAVE ANY CLIFF'S NOTES FOR THE 'FOR DUMMIES' BOOKS?
BOOKSTORE
TOM WILSON & TOM II

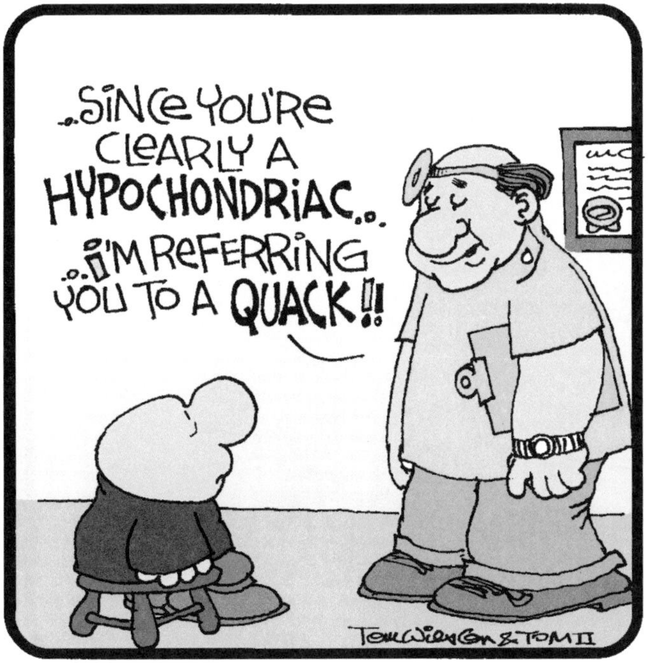
..SINCE YOU'RE CLEARLY A HYPOCHONDRIAC.. ..I'M REFERRING YOU TO A QUACK!!
TOM WILSON & TOM II

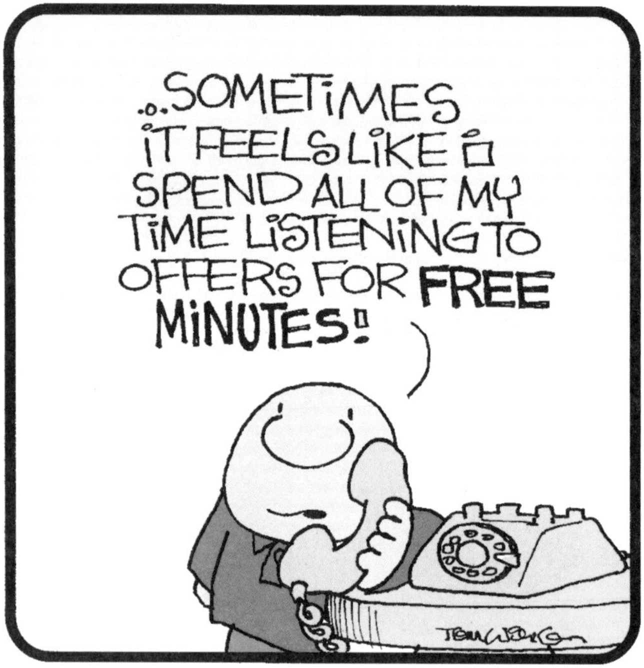
..SOMETIMES IT FEELS LIKE I SPEND ALL OF MY TIME LISTENING TO OFFERS FOR FREE MINUTES!

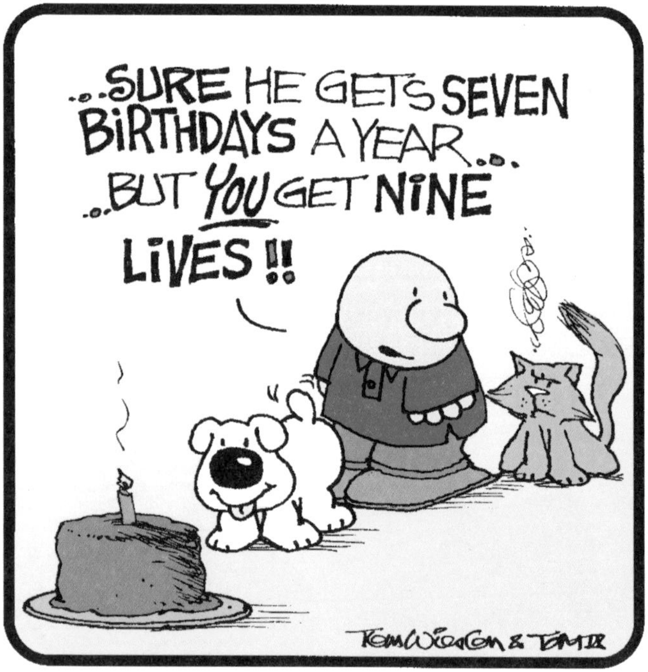
..SURE HE GETS SEVEN BIRTHDAYS A YEAR... ..BUT YOU GET NINE LIVES!!

?
?
„YOU DON'T GET ANY POINTS FOR THAT."
13
RULES

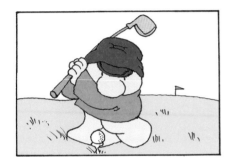

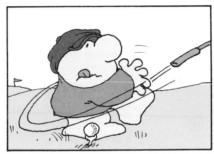

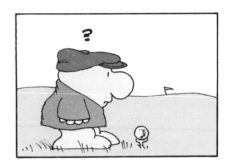

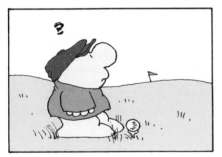

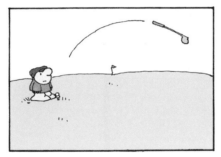

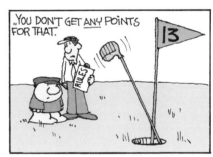

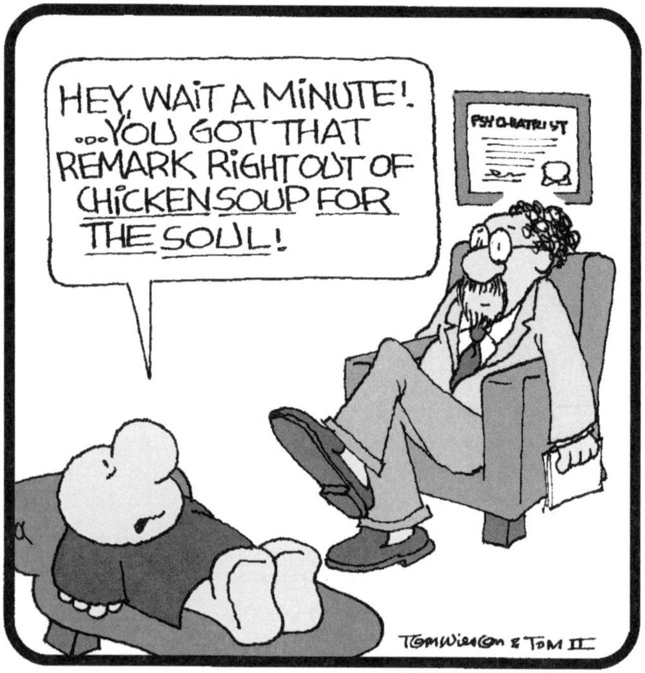
HEY, WAIT A MINUTE! ...YOU GOT THAT REMARK RIGHT OUT OF CHICKEN SOUP FOR THE SOUL!
PSYCHIATRIST

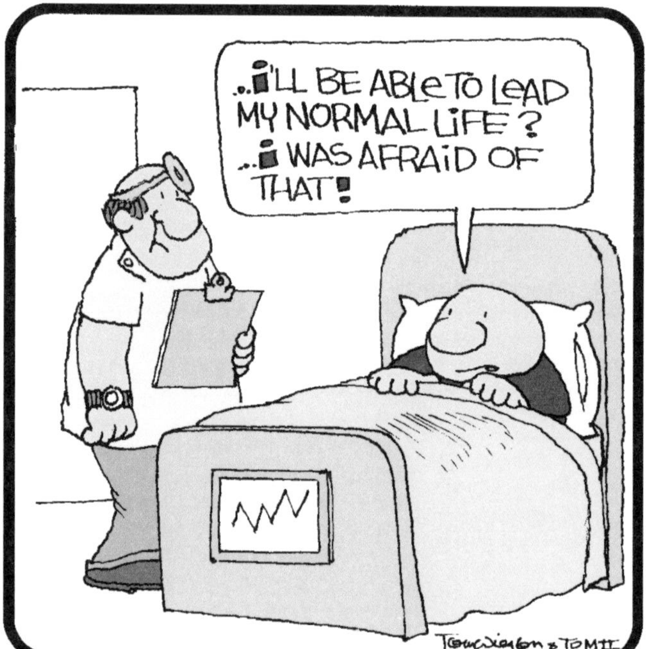
..I'LL BE ABLE TO LEAD MY NORMAL LIFE? ..I WAS AFRAID OF THAT!

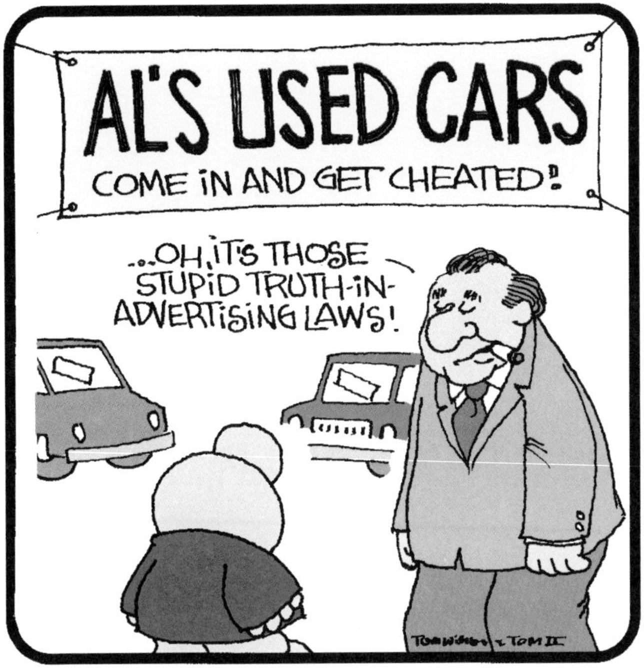
AL'S USED CARS
COME IN AND GET CHEATED!
...OH, IT'S THOSE STUPID TRUTH-IN-ADVERTISING LAWS!
TOM WILSON & TOM II

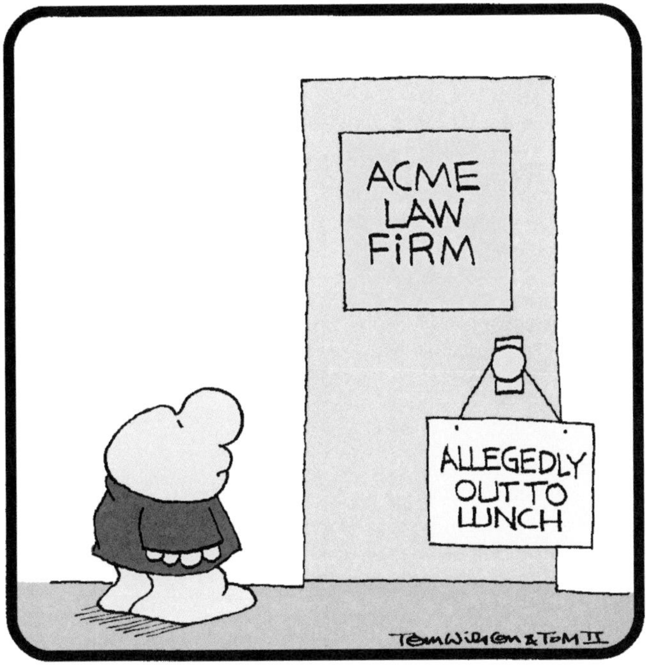
ACME LAW FIRM
ALLEGEDLY OUT TO LUNCH
TOM WILSON & TOM II

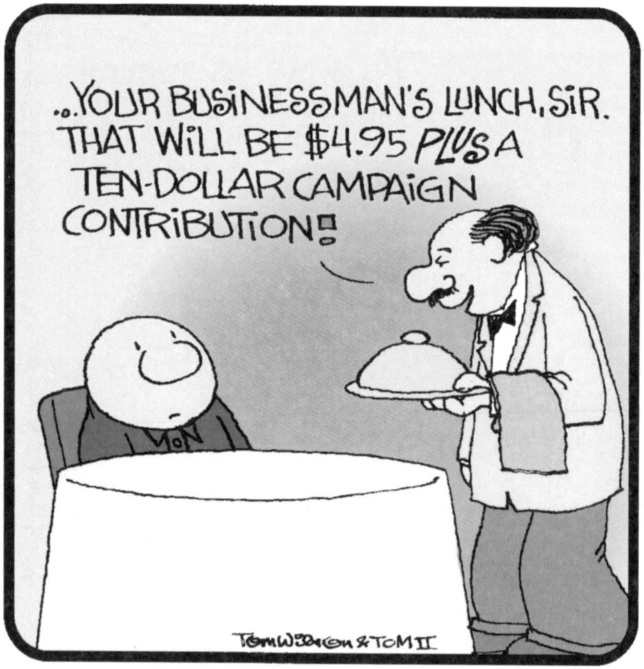
..YOUR BUSINESSMAN'S LUNCH, SIR. THAT WILL BE $4.95 PLUS A TEN-DOLLAR CAMPAIGN CONTRIBUTION!!
MON
TOM WILSON & TOM II

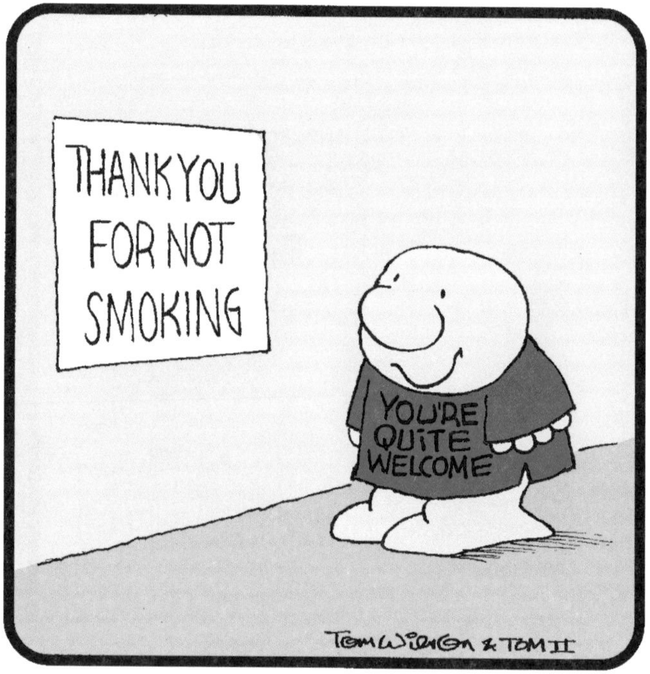
THANK YOU FOR NOT SMOKING
YOU'RE QUITE WELCOME
TOM WILSON & TOM II

SKRITCH
SKRATCH
FLUMP
...ALL OF HIS FLEAS JUMPED AT ONCE!

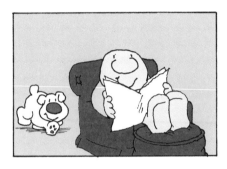

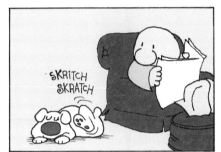

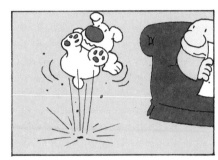

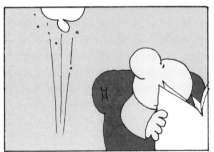

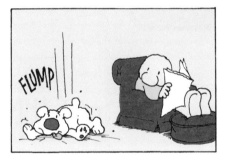

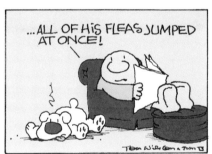

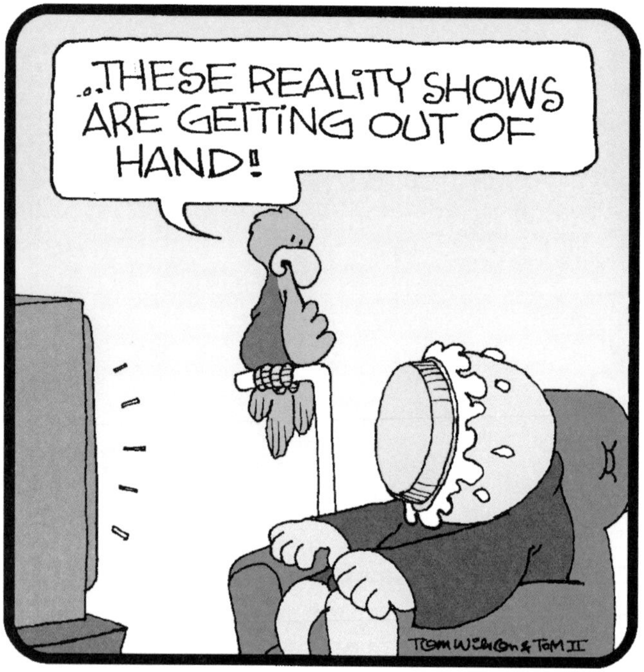
..THESE REALITY SHOWS ARE GETTING OUT OF HAND!
TOM WILSON & TOM II

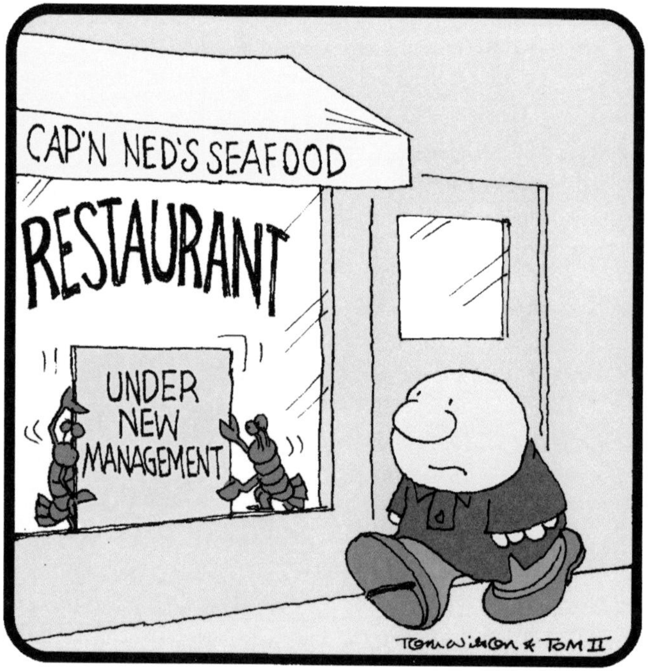
CAP'N NED'S SEAFOOD
RESTAURANT
UNDER NEW MANAGEMENT
TOM WILSON & TOM II

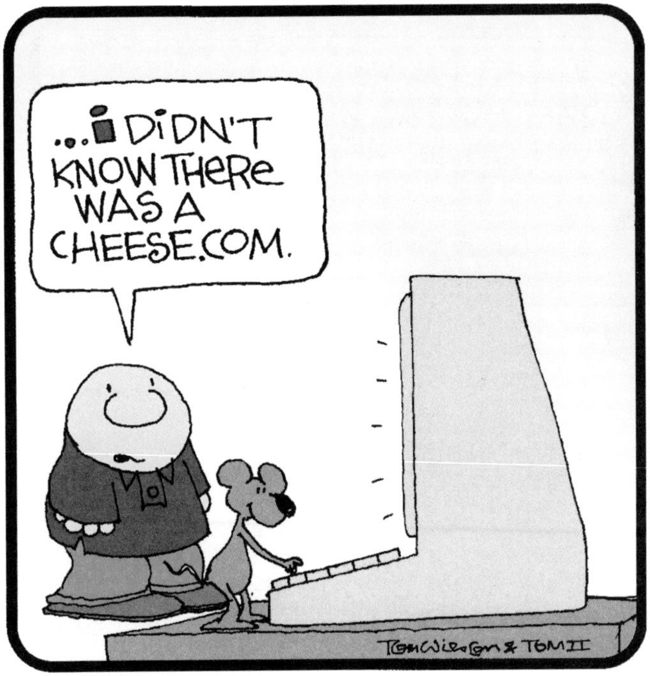
...I DIDN'T KNOW THERE WAS A CHEESE.COM.
Tom Wilson & Tom II

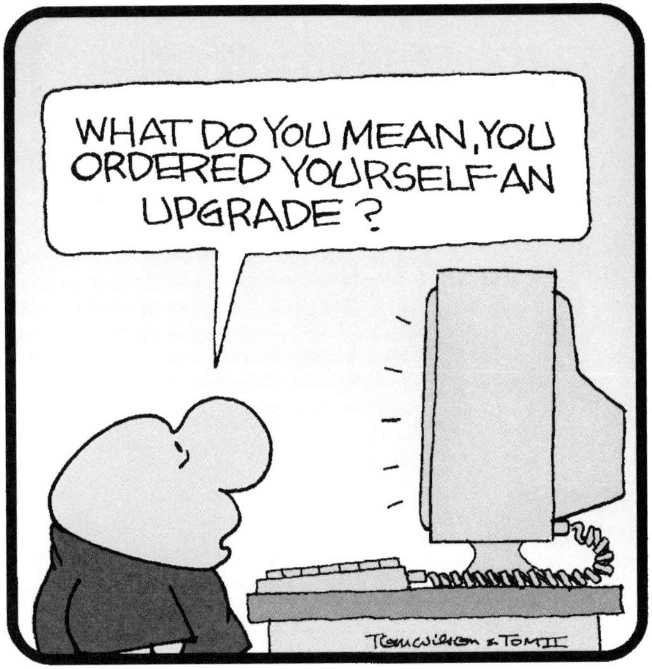
WHAT DO YOU MEAN, YOU ORDERED YOURSELF AN UPGRADE?
Tom Wilson & Tom II

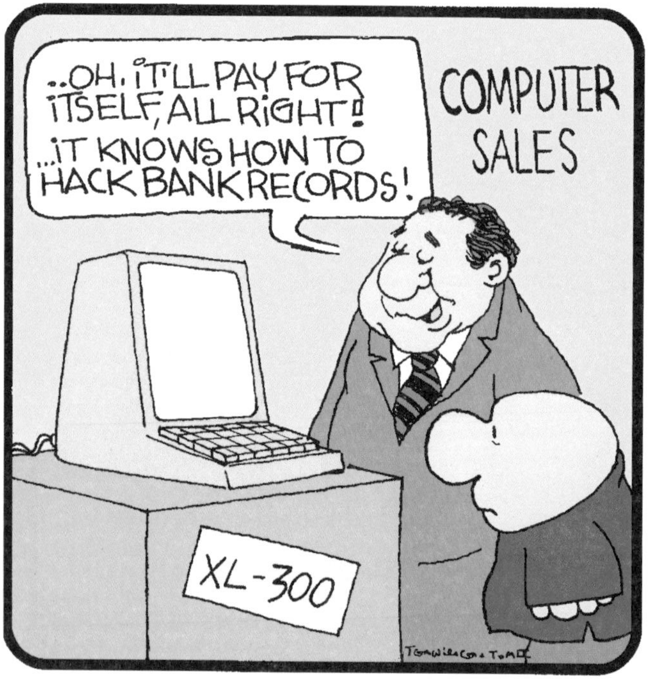
..OH, IT'LL PAY FOR ITSELF, ALL RIGHT! ...IT KNOWS HOW TO HACK BANK RECORDS!
COMPUTER SALES
XL-300

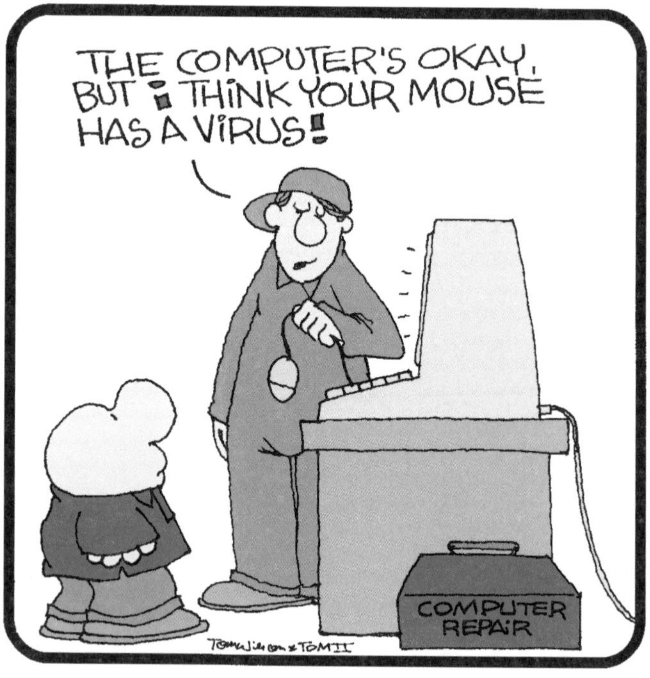
THE COMPUTER'S OKAY, BUT I THINK YOUR MOUSE HAS A VIRUS!
COMPUTER REPAIR

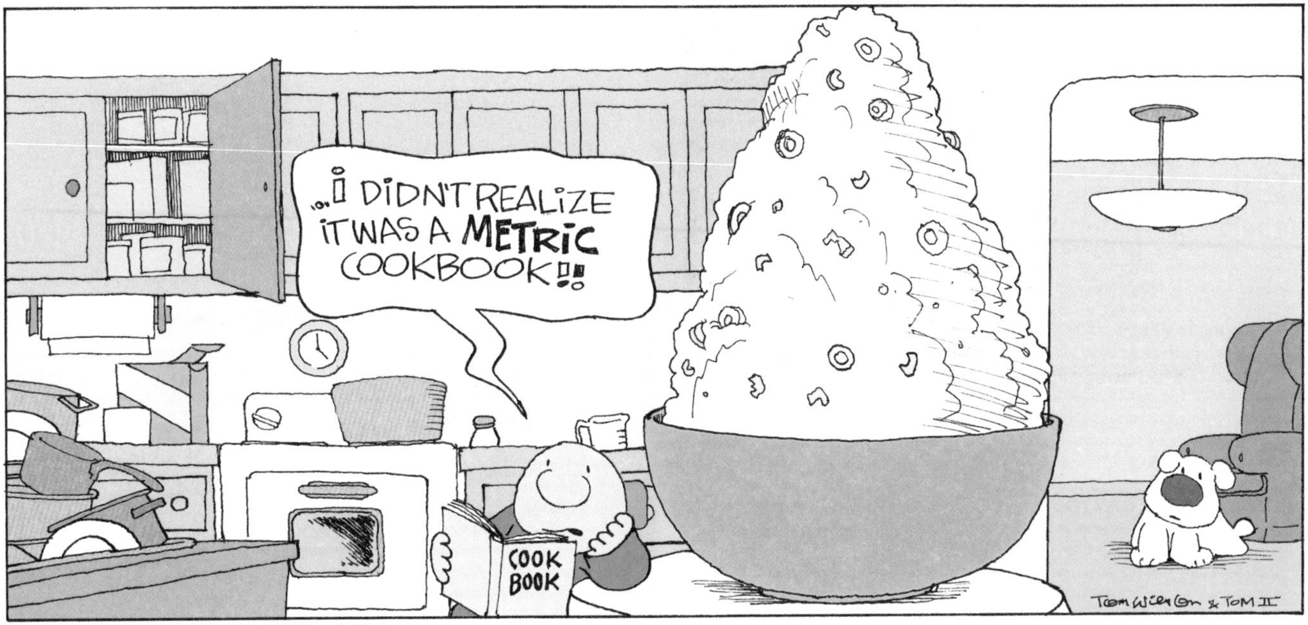
...I DIDN'T REALIZE IT WAS A METRIC COOKBOOK!!
COOK BOOK
Tom Wilson & TOM II

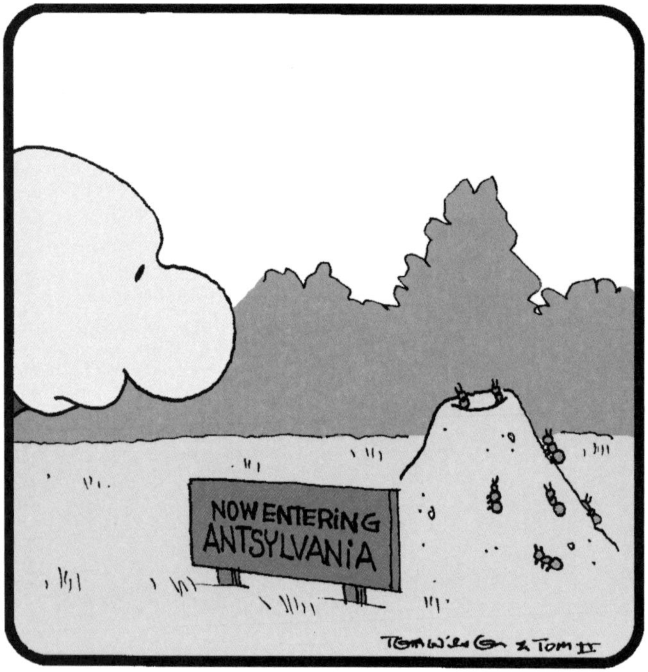
NOW ENTERING
ANTSYLVANIA
TOM WILSON & TOM II

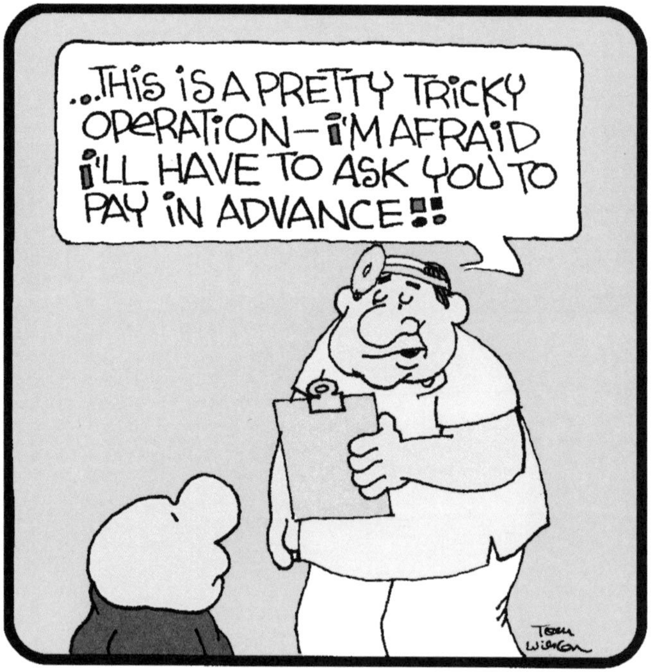
..THIS IS A PRETTY TRICKY OPERATION— I'M AFRAID I'LL HAVE TO ASK YOU TO PAY IN ADVANCE!!
TOM WILSON

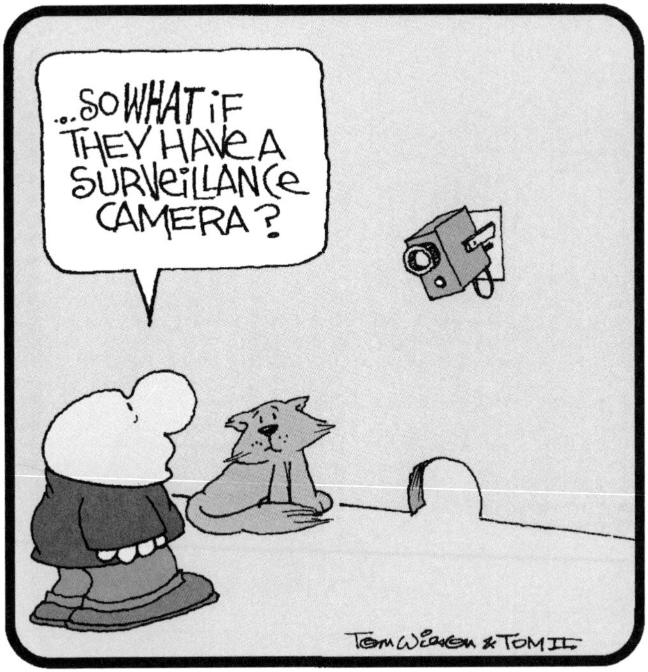
...SO WHAT IF THEY HAVE A SURVEILLANCE CAMERA?
Tom Wilson & Tom II

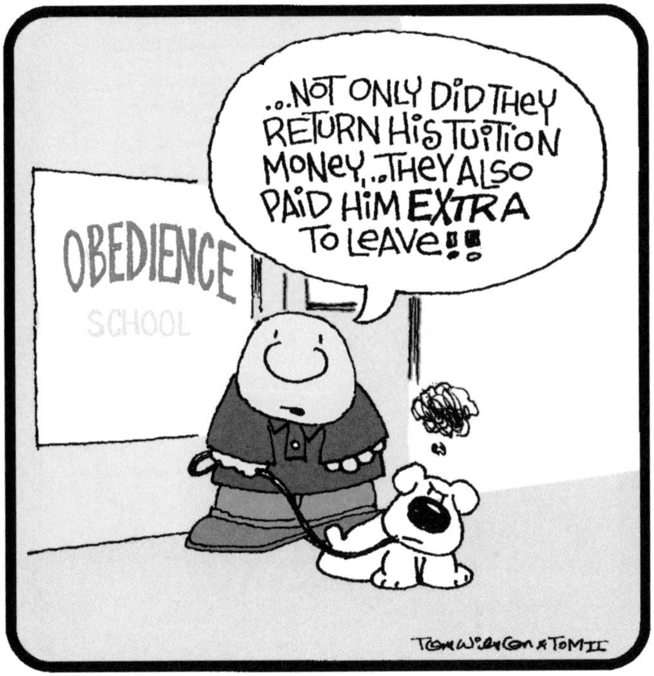
OBEDIENCE
SCHOOL
...NOT ONLY DID THEY RETURN HIS TUITION MONEY,...THEY ALSO PAID HIM EXTRA TO LEAVE!!
Tom Wilson & Tom II

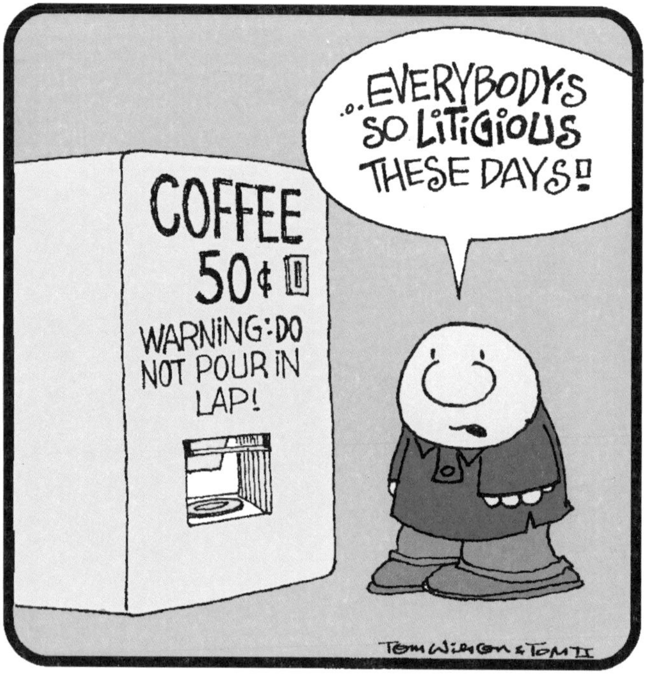
COFFEE
50¢
WARNING: DO NOT POUR IN LAP!
...EVERYBODY'S SO LITIGIOUS THESE DAYS!
TOM WILSON & TOM II

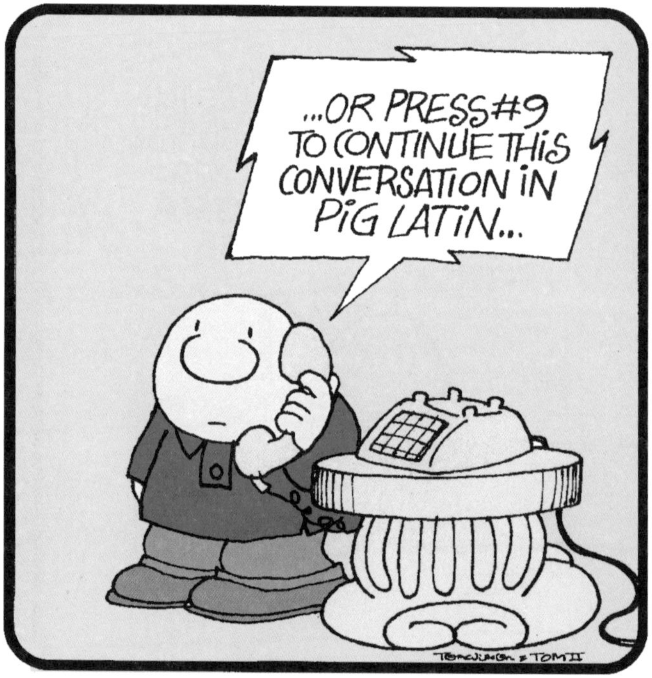
...OR PRESS #9 TO CONTINUE THIS CONVERSATION IN PIG LATIN...
TOM WILSON & TOM II